A GLASS BOUQUET

BY

SANDY BROWN

AUTHOR OF " ANGELS DO TELL LIES "

And " ICE COLD REVENGE"

This heartrending story is a work of fiction based on true life experience.

For all the children out there who are scarred by the past.

Your future is what you make it.

Have hope!

One day at a time, this is enough.

Do not look back and grieve over the past for it is gone.

And do not be troubled about the future for it has not yet come.

Live in the present!

And make it so beautiful it will be worth remembering.

CHAPTER ONE

The early morning sunshine squeezed himself through the chink in Libby's bedroom curtains, and rested upon her sleeping eyelids. She stirred, half smiling as she felt his warm glow on her face. She didn't mind at all that her friend the sun wouldn't let her sleep this morning. The half awake thoughts swimming around in her head were pleasant ones for a change, exaggerated visions of a Grand Ball, with the girls in their Prom dresses and Libby, the Queen of them all! You see, last night she and her foster carer Maria, had sat together making great plans for Libby's eighteenth birthday party. This was a big one, a special one. It represented freedom, she could vote, she could drink, stay out late, Oh! The list was endless, but it also meant much more than this for Libby. It heralded the end of a long and at times difficult relationship with Social Services. Becoming eighteen, an adult therefore, would also mean no more reviews, no more medicals – Yuk! And maybe, just maybe she would get to see her family after all this time.

These exciting thoughts gave Libby a burst of unprecedented energy, as she threw back the duvet and thanked the Sun for waking her so gently. She wasn't even angry today that the curtains never quite closed properly; otherwise he would not have been able to enter and remind her of what a beautiful day it was going to be. She put on her dressing gown and slippers gave her hair a quick little ruffle with her hand and yawned the sleepiness out of her body as she hopped down the stairs. The senses in her nose were now awakening and following the aroma of bacon and eggs sizzling in the pan on the kitchen stove.

"Good morning!" She yawned once more as she wandered over to the fridge and poured herself an oversized glass of orange juice, drinking it as though she were drinking in the golden Sun itself.

"Sleep well?" Enquired Maria.

"Absolutely, I had wonderful dreams which have given me some great ideas for the party!" said Libby with renewed energy.

"Hey, slow down, there *are* limits you know. You're not Cinderella and there's no Prince Charming on the horizon." Smiled Maria.

"*I* know" said Libby, "But it's all *so* exciting and I just want to enjoy all the plans before university." Libby lowered her voice, at the thought of a different kind of struggle ahead of her. She had worked so very hard to achieve her G.C.S.E's and left school with ten of them and good grades too, outstanding for a child in care by all accounts. Libby knew that this had been largely due to the encouragement given her by Maria and her husband Robert Sinclair.

They had fostered Libby when she was eight years old, an endearing little child and very pretty. In the beginning Robert and Maria had no idea how long Libby would be with them. She was then, still young enough to have been adopted, but Maria and Robert had fallen in love with her. She settled into their family very quickly and it felt, to all of them, as though she had always been there, and though they had two daughters of their own, in their hearts Libby was little different.

It had been so hard in the beginning when Libby moved in. It wasn't known whether adoptive parents would be found but as time went by, Libby had taken to the family so well and the placement became so stable, that long-term fostering with the Sinclair family was eventually considered to be the best option. Once the Permanence Panel had given the final seal of approval, everyone could breathe a sigh of relief, knowing that Libby would be staying until she was eighteen – or maybe even longer! Although Robert and Maria's daughters, Harriet and Fiona were now at university, they too had always loved Libby like they would have had she been their own sister.

Libby had lived a very privileged lifestyle for the past ten years; very different from the one she'd lived with her birth family prior to being taken into care. Maria was a solicitor with a small firm in the village and Robert was a Bank Manager in a nearby small town. They lived a very comfortable existence in their rural setting, owning a magnificent old house at the end of a long winding lane in the middle of nowhere. Libby loved living in the Derbyshire countryside. It was in stark contrast to the very rundown council estate she had endured in the city with her birth family all those years ago when she was very small. It was hard to believe that the venue of her old life wasn't so very far away geographically from her present one. In fact it was less than twenty miles away in Sheffield. She would often reflect on the way things used to be. The coldness when there was no heating in the cramped flat. The hunger when there was no food in the cupboards, but worst of all, when there was no love to be wrapped around her for comfort, when her parents had spent the entire day in bed chasing their booze and drug induced dreams.

"No!" That was enough reflection for today. Libby didn't want her thoughts of the old life, invading her present one, especially not today. Nothing could spoil her happiness and excitement. Maria had noticed the dark mood briefly descend upon Libby. She always knew by her facial expression when it was with her, over the years. She had become attuned, as most mothers would be to their children's feelings.

"Hey Libby!" Said Maria with great enthusiasm. "When you've finished breakfast why don't you ring Polly and tell her the good news?"

"Oh good idea" splattered Libby, her mouth so filled with the bacon and egg butty Maria had made for her, that the words had no space to form in there. Licking her greasy fingers, she negotiated her way around the kitchen table with a mug of tea in her free hand and made her way into the lounge where she could sit comfortably to talk on the 'phone, perhaps for hours. Naughty really, knowing how Maria would disapprove of her licked fingers grasping the receiver without being washed. Libby eased herself back into the cushions and draped her legs over the chair arm, as she dialled Polly's number. Maria smiled and shook her head as she returned to the dishes she had piled into the dishwasher, content enough that her foster child – soon to be an adult, was deliriously happy today.

She could hear the giggles drifting from the lounge, like little glossy bubbles floating and popping in the air as Libby's call was answered.

"Hi Poll, it's me!" Libby sat back in the armchair to enjoy her conversation with her sister.

CHAPTER TWO

Polly was Libby's sister and about a year younger than Libby. She too was in foster care, with Sally and John. However, in sharp contrast, the Dawsons lived in the bustling centre of the big city. It was a nice enough area of Sheffield and a very neat council estate, where most of the neighbours were friendly, very down-to-earth 'Townies'. Polly loved it as she was quite a different character to Libby, not so 'airy-fairy 'as she herself so eloquently put it. She loved sport and Sally and John had encouraged her to join trampoline club and the after-school all girls football matches at the school she had recently left which was just at the end of the street.

On this lovely sunny morning, Sally had waved John off to work and was sighing at the tardiness of her two small sons, Bruce and Billy, as they were now still in their pyjamas enjoying the feathery mess of a pillow fight between the bunks in their bedroom, despite Sally's pleas for them to wash and dress.

Polly was oblivious to all the noise, she had grown used to it over time, it had always been a busy household, but there was a lot of love and happiness here. There was a kind of happy-go-lucky atmosphere, yet at the same time there were firm boundaries set in place, and Sally ensured that everyone understood them clearly.

As the 'phone rang, Sally's hands were deeply entrenched in a huge lump of dough as she began today's bread making process.

"Polly!" she called, "Could you get that love? I am rather indisposed just now!" she sang, in her pseudo-posh voice, with a cheeky smile on her round rosy face.

Polly was in the sitting room stretched out across the rug on her stomach, her lower legs raised in the air with ankles crossed. She didn't hear Sally the first time, her mind had wandered into the world of the T.V. screen whilst her thumbs dexterously and expertly caressed the play station. As Sally called again, more forcefully, her instruction began to filter through along with the shrill ringing of the telephone, and as Polly retrieved her mind from the game, she reached out for the intruding receiver.

"Hello?" she said with an intentionally grumpy tone. She wasn't happy at having to break from her game and enforce the real world upon her brain, but she *had* obeyed Sally's request.

"Hi Poll, it's me!" the voice shrieked. Polly knew by the usual greeting who 'Me'. Was.

"Oh Hi" replied Polly, the anticipation now gone as she realised it was her sister – again!

"Hey guess what Poll? I'm having a party for my eighteenth in a few weeks. It's going to be a masked ball, with fairy lights and music and……………."

By now the words were meaningless to Polly. This was Libby, she was off again in her dream world where everything was perfect and everyone lived happily ever after with a mummy and a daddy and two point four children, in a lovely suburban home (a bit like Libby's house I suppose!) but Polly was more pessimistic, the past had left a much deeper imprint on her mind and she knew life wasn't always kind.

Despite being younger than Libby, Polly had a more practical outlook on life. Was this perhaps the two different lives they had with their respective foster families, or was it just personality? Polly often reflected, as did Libby, on her previous life, perhaps even more so than her sister, maybe she was more adversely affected, or was Libby just very expert at concealing her true feelings, with her airy-fairy ways? Polly had tried very hard indeed to be non-judgemental of her birth mother, but she had been a child and half the time was either completely oblivious, *or* protected by others from what had really been happening. The two girls always referred to their birth parent as Tracey. Almost as though the very title of 'mother' was a mismatch and was impossible for them to relate to. They had talked together many times and had attempted to show juvenile empathy for her situation, but the pain they had endured was always strong enough to dissipate any excuses they could find.

14

"Yeah, yeah, anyway Lib' I've got to go now I'm a bit busy at the minute, but yes, I'd love to come to your party, maybe we could meet up in town for coffee and a chat about it. Bye!"

Polly had very quickly become bored with Libby's ramblings about Prom dresses and cakes and masks! She wanted to get back to her game and the oblivion it gave her from her memories.

Growing up, both Libby and Polly had been quite fortunate given their circumstances. Sally and Maria had communicated well with each other regarding the girls, despite being two very different people. They had promoted and supervised regular contact, encouraging sleepovers, thus ensuring they grew up being part of each other's lives, enjoying normal sibling rivalry. Materially, Libby's life was more privileged as Robert and Maria were a professional couple and their circle of friends and business acquaintances were likewise. Robert was content to sink into his big armchair at the end of a busy day at the bank, and read his newspaper. Maria worked part-time and loved to come home from the office or a day in court and potter around the garden, carefully choosing and cutting fresh blooms in order to show off her flower arranging skills, carefully slotting the long-stemmed roses into her antique crystal vases. She would place her roses on top of her highly polished piano, lovingly caressing their perfect velvety heads with her manicured hands. Closing her eyes she would lift her head and breathe in their scent. She would stroll out onto the balcony and allow her eyes to enjoy the scenery beyond, the quaint little village of Bradwell nestling below and the lush fields stretching like a rippling green blanket all around, giving comfort. All this with which to indulge her senses.

Sally on the other hand, was the 'mother earth' type. She had a wicked sense of humour and a wonderful gift with food. She loved food, loved cooking and baking for her little family but most of all she loved baking bread. John was a postman, and usually had a very energetic day, effectively walking miles and therefore, easily walking off the calories consumed from Sally's scrumptious bread. Their garden was very basic; a plain well cut lawn, with a trampoline at the very bottom for the boys and a wooden picket fence on either side informing the occupants of the boundary between them and their neighbours. The lawn was littered with little toy cars, buckets and spades lay half buried in the sand pit in the corner and brightly coloured footballs sat here and there, waiting to be sent on a journey through the air to land who knows where. However, there was a little corner by the kitchen door with a white though weathered P.V.C. table and chairs which Polly usually occupied with her homework on a sunny day. Yet despite their obvious lifestyle differences, the two foster families had got along quite well and both had made effort and sacrifice to allow the girls to grow up together.

Now, Maria needed Sally more than ever. She had plans for Libby's eighteenth birthday party that would be kept secret from the girls. It was going to be a difficult task for Maria and she would need Sally's co-operation but with her experience and professional contacts she had high hopes of pulling off something that was perhaps virtually unknown in the fostering world.

CHAPTER THREE

It was mid-afternoon and Libby had spent the last hour sitting on the balcony, making a list, a very long list, of all the guests she was going to invite to her party. It was the only thing on Libby's mind twent-four-seven. It was all she could talk about and everyone was tiring of her incessant chatter. When her list was complete and covered two whole pages of her notebook, Libby put down her pen and sat back sipping from her glass of cold lemonade. Her mind was momentarily distracted as she watched her friend the Sun playing and dancing his shadows across the green hills, changing their shapes and colours as the little clouds fleetingly eclipsed his rays then sped on their way. Sitting here alone, the dark thoughts once more crept deviously into Libby's head, almost as though they were trying to evict the good thoughts and claim the space they occupied, in an endeavour to engulf and persuade her mind to sink into total despair. It's so very strange how these thoughts could infiltrate considering what a good and happy life Libby had enjoyed for the greater part of her existence. Yet she couldn't help remembering her early days now and then. She had been so very very unhappy. She could almost feel the cold of the bedroom she had shared with *all* of her siblings. In this grim damp room with no curtains and just a thin old duvet, the only warmth available was from each other. She and Polly shared the top bunk and would cling to each other through the night, not only for shared bodily warmth, but also for the comfort it gave them to know they had each other for protection against the terrible shouting they could hear emanating from the living room. Most nights there had been no supper and their little bellies ached from hunger as they shivered in the darkness. The only visual comfort came from the warm yellow light of the streetlamp situated on the pavement outside their window as it shone its golden glow through the grimy bare glass pane. The two older brothers Scott and Jared didn't fare so well either, as they shared the lower bunk, and being bigger and older they'd had less space, sleeping top to toe and had therefore less duvet to cover each of them. Their greatest argument each night had been about who was hogging most of this one grubby duvet, each of them in turn tugging at it to ensure it reached his chin in order to keep the cold at bay, until the cheap and dirty fabric was beginning to rip in the middle. Libby had repeatedly told them to shut up so that everyone could get to sleep and assured them that pretty soon the duvet would rip clean across the middle and then, they would have only half of a duvet each. The baby, Beth, slept in a rather grubby second-hand cot in the corner. Sleeping was a rarity for her too, as the mattress stunk of urine and her nappy was firmly fixed to her nether regions until morning, so wet and sodden that it would simply disintegrate when removed, but mum Tracy, and dad Darren would not allow their slumbers to be disturbed for something as unnecessary as changing a nappy.

There were times when the older children were so hungry, they would brave the freezing cold, and creep downstairs in the dead of night, carefully manoeuvring around the creaky floorboards, into the living room and devour the cold chips and battered fish skin left behind on the greasy paper, the remains of mum and dad's fish supper. The congealed cold grease would cling to their teeth but they could wash it all down with the dregs of cold tea left in the cups. The beer cans were always totally empty. Never was there a drop of liquid left in those! They would then creep quietly back to bed, their stomachs nauseatingly full.

The days had not been much better. Their parents would be sleeping through oblivion well into the middle of the afternoon. The children would rise late too, having had little sleep through the night, too late to go to school. Understandably they would then be reluctant to endure the scorn of their teachers for turning in late, so it was the lesser of two evils to stay at home. Besides, how could you go out with socks that didn't match no underwear to be found and only one shoe making itself available just when you need to run out the door?

The house was a total shambles; in fact it was a disaster zone. There was no adult supervision when the young ones were trying to put together the makings of a meal from whatever they could find. Surprising how good sugar from the jar or dry stale bread can taste when there's nothing else to be found, and the green mouldy bits were especially tasty. Perhaps the antibiotic effect of this was what prevented the entire family from going down with all sorts of diseases, though they all drew the line at chewing on the cigarette ends which were ground into the carpet and clinging to the greasy patches. The baby was not so fortunate however. Not yet able to walk or be independent, she would scream uncontrollably whilst her parents slept away their day in the next room, the drugs and alcohol providing *them* with a blissful, unconscious slumber.

Their father Darren didn't work of course. He constantly rattled on about his 'bad back', and how he had to manage to bring up his family on benefits because he was 'disabled you know!' However, there was always money for cigarettes and beer. Cider was mum's choice of beverage, *and* it was a bit cheaper than beer therefore she could drink more of it. The baby had permanently dewy eyes and frown lines adorned her little face, so sad at such a young age. Her life so far, appeared to be a mirror image of the others. As Libby reflected, it saddened her to now realise how Beth must have felt in her tiny immature mind. The image of Beth's little face flashed into her head as she reflected on those huge tear filled eyes, fractured by the presence of the bars on her cot, almost like an infant inmate of her personal little prison.

Suddenly and without warning the bells of Bradwell church clock peeled the hour. Libby hated the church bells, but it was enough to snap her out of her black mood and the dark thoughts she had harboured dissipated as her eyes fell upon the little houses of the village below. The cottages with their thick stone walls, the new estate on the fringes, the church clock tower pointing skywards toward heaven, like a finger reminding everyone where God lived and more to the point that he was ever watching our every move.

Libby decided she needed to take a walk to clear her mind, and with a shout of "Be back shortly!" She grabbed her coat and left the house. As she emerged once more, into the outside air her friend the Sun clothed her with warmth as he rested his comforting, glowing shawl around her shoulders and she realised that she hadn't needed her coat after all, it was just the dark cold images in her head which had physically affected her and made her shiver. She walked slowly down the lane, totally in love with summer. The cuckoo was calling in the distance and the little brook that ran through the village was hastily meandering on its adventures to who knows where, and babbling the village gossip to everyone as it passed on its way. She stood on the bridge for a moment listening to its peaceful comforting sound, gazing at the quiet hills, and in that moment she asked herself why she had felt so sad, when after all, she had a good life now, in glorious surroundings, yet there *was* something missing, though she was puzzled as to what that elusive 'thing' was.

'This is silly' she thought to herself. I have so much to look forward to! She turned quickly on her heels and skipped her way along the path passing the bakery and the convenience store. She called Hi!" to Mr. Miller behind the counter as she passed. She was heading for the Post Office on the main street, to buy invitations and postage stamps to get started on her quest for the 'Party of the Year'. Mr. Johnson was busy unpacking a new delivery that day, but willingly stopped in order to help Libby with her choice. After very careful consideration and much negotiation with Mr. Johnson, Libby decided upon some very tasteful white cards with little gold champagne bottles releasing an effervescence of tiny gold bubbles, and two crossed champagne glasses across the corner, with an embossed gold '18' at the top. Maria had taught her how to choose things wisely and how to take into account what was fitting. These, she thought, Maria would approve of.

On her way home Libby made a conscious effort to put all thoughts of the past out of her head and enjoy planning her forthcoming event.

CHAPTER FOUR

Maria had a huge task ahead of her and as she sat at her desk at work, she pushed her hand through her dark fringe, and let out a breathy sigh. Even with her legal experience she knew she would have to play detective big time in order to pull off her plan successfully. If they are lucky, foster carers are given a chronology of the child's background when they are placed with them, perhaps a family tree and an update periodically regarding the current situation with the birth family, though as Libby and Polly had no family contact whatsoever, current information was sadly lacking. If they are not lucky they may be given little information at all. This was the first action Maria decided to take which would set the wheels in motion as she picked up the 'phone to call Libby's social worker.

"Good morning!" she chirped with her best professional telephone manner. "May I speak to Grace Marsden please, its Maria Sinclair speaking regarding Libby McIntyre. Maria *was* extremely professional at everything she did. Whether that be her part-time job with the Firm, her care of her daughters and Libby, or planning an exceptional dinner party for friends and colleagues and *this* project would be no exception, it would need all the precision of a military coup, so much so that her head swam with the enormity of it. Just as she was beginning to tire of 'We're Walking in the Air' ringing in her ears having been placed on 'hold,' the voice of Grace Marsden broke the monotony

"Hi Maria, how are you? Long time no see!" she warbled in her pseudo sing-song manner.

"Good morning" replied Maria curtly. It's because I haven't heard from you for a while that I'm ringing! First of all I would really like a current update on the situation with Libby's birth family. She's grown up now, eighteen in a few weeks as you know, and I honestly feel that her past is beginning to catch up with her. I've noticed her day dreaming quite frequently and it leaves her in a low mood. Perhaps if I could give her some news of her birth family it may give her some hope of future contact with her parents or her siblings."

There was a deafening silence as Maria waited for a reply.

"To be honest Maria, its really not good news."

Another silence.

"Well, surely any news is better than none, Maria smiled spuriously to herself and to Grace's imaginary face. She was used to the fact that information didn't always filter through immediately, but she urgently wanted to know *how* serious it was and why she hadn't been informed sooner. More to the point, who was going to tell Libby, *whatever* it was.

"The fact is................"

Another pause which was now beginning to frustrate Maria. 'For goodness sake! Why doesn't the woman just spit it out' she thought to herself in her no-nonsense way.

"Well." Grace's voice was now hesitant and Maria could detect with her professionalism, that she was almost gritting her teeth in a vain attempt to keep the words swimming around in her mouth, not allowing them the freedom to be expressed. "Well, I may as well tell you. The girls' mother, Tracey is in prison I'm afraid, I've been meaning to ring you to let you know, but you know how it is."

'At last!' Thought Maria. She had finally allowed the words to fly along the air-waves. "Yes, yes" spluttered Maria hastily, as Grace waffled on and on about the mountain of paper work on her desk and the hundreds of 'phone calls she had to make.

"But getting back to Tracey, *why* is she in prison Grace? It's just that I'm planning Libby's eighteenth birthday party and I began thinking that perhaps we could do something to make it easier and happier for her, perhaps even a card. Would Tracey send her a card? How long will she be in prison do you think?" Maria's anxious questions were racing ahead, her voice still elegant like a racehorse trying to reach the post, yet still looking poised and beautiful.

"Let me stop you right there Maria, unfortunately Tracey will be inside for a very long time. She's in for murder!"

Maria froze in her chair; the receiver had become welded to her hand. This was big, this was *huge*, and her only thoughts were of how she was going to tell Libby – *and* Sally – *and* Polly!

"Please Grace, stop waffling and tell me exactly what has happened. I have a right to know, I *care* for this child emotionally as well as physically. I, we, need all the information in order to prepare her and Polly for what the future holds for them, for the family!"

"Well, that's not all Maria I'm afraid. Tracey killed her husband, Darren, the girls' father!"

Both of them fell into a silence. It was as though the words carried some sort of virus which paralysed their mouths.

"Maria? Maria are you there? "Stammered Grace fearfully.

"Yes! I'm here she whispered.

"Look, I realise what a shock this must be to you. Perhaps it would be better if I mail you a chronology of everything so that you can read it at your leisure, you'll be able to take it in easier. O.k.! I'll talk to you soon." It felt almost as though Grace couldn't wait to get off the 'phone.

"Leisure!" Sneered Maria angrily, "Since when do I have time for leisure?" Then, as always, she regretted her angry thoughts. She was of the opinion that being a social worker must be worse than being a solicitor. Poor Grace must be absolutely snowed under with work. These poor social workers had little in the way of resources, and therefore had heavy case loads to deal with. Also she realised what a dreadful piece of news it was to pass on, and how difficult it must have been to express.

Suddenly she realised that she herself needed to share all of this with Sally. She knew from past experience that this was what was expected of her. Although it was not her responsibility, it usually meant that the two foster carers could decide a mutual plan of action, depending on the situation, in order that the outcome for the girls was as good as they could make it. Many families had skeletons in their cupboards, but this was an entire wardrobe full! At this moment, it escaped Maria as to how on earth they could work round this one. However, she picked up the 'phone, dialled Sally's number, and asked her to sit down.

A week later, a large brown envelope was delivered. It bore the red ink frank mark of Social Services and on the flap it was stamped 'PRIVATE AND CONFIDENTIAL'. It was always cock-eyed this stamp, Maria thought to herself, almost as though it was a distraction from the overwhelming temptation to rip it open there and then, but Maria knew what it would be.

Libby spotted it as she came down to breakfast that morning. "Ah! Is that about me by any chance?" she queried, with expectation in her voice. The only things on her mind these days being her party and college.

"I expect so." said Maria with a forced smile on her face. She knew what the envelope would contain and wasn't going to open it until everyone had left the house for work or college. She needed to be alone to read this one, to be able to digest every word. Maria had dealt with many traumas both in her career as a solicitor and in her life as a foster carer, but never anything like this, in this sleepy little village. What would the village residents make of all this. Bradwell was a quaint little place with its babbling brook, its idle village gossip about who was going out with who or the new coat that Mrs. Smith was wearing to church on Sunday. How would they cope with *this*? Then it sensibly occurred to Maria that they need never know. This was highly confidential and hopefully would never emerge.

The very second everyone had gone through the door and the house had fallen into an eerie silent sleep once more, Maria ripped open the large brown envelope sitting on the table. She was so eager to browse its contents that she almost tore the batch of papers within it. She pulled the white sheets from their brown sleeve, and cast the envelope aside allowing it to float to the kitchen floor, as if it were glad to be free of its heavy burden. It *was* a heavy burden indeed in more than a physical sense. Maria felt she needed a cup of strong Earl Grey tea in order to fortify her resolve and proceeded to go through the motions of tea-making like an automaton, without thought, or sight, unable to take her eyes from the material in her hand. Her body became heavier as her eyes scanned the pages, so much so that her bottom found its way onto the seat of a dining chair, without direction or conscious effort. She knew the project she had started wasn't going to be easy but *this* really was not a good beginning.

The instant she had read the last word, Maria knew she must call Sally to discuss this revelation yet in her usual positive manner Maria consoled her internal world by assuring herself that things couldn't get any worse!

Sally picked up the receiver of her ringing 'phone. Reluctantly she held it to her ear and quietly said "Hello?"

"Hi Sally, it's me, Maria." Her tone was sombre. The kind of dark tone almost of bereavement, yet that was quite fitting under the circumstances.

"I would imagine you have received your copy of the paperwork this morning Sally. We need to get our heads together regarding the girls, about how, and what, we are going to tell them."

"I know." Replied Sally with a heavy sadness. As the conversation continued between these two caring women, the full sad story unfolded. Between them they picked out the bare bones from the endless pages each of them held. Both Sally and Maria knew beforehand that Tracey may be in prison for a long time if the charge was murder but the full horror of the facts before them brought new meaning to the outcome for Libby and Polly, *and* of course, their siblings.

CHAPTER FIVE

As Tracey languished in her cold prison cell, she would often lie on her frugal metal framed bed and allow her mind to wander through a cruel journey of her past. She and Darren had practically grown up together in the back streets of Sheffield. They had lived on opposite sides of a tiny cobbled street, with a continuous row of back-to-back terraced houses running down each side like two brick ribbons framing the rough cobbled centre. As children they had played on these cobbles, occasionally dodging any traffic which may venture through, and if it rained, they would play hopscotch in the passageways which joined the pairs of little houses and led to the back yards.

With little spare money available for fun and activities, Tracey and Darren were thrown together in their own little world, and were rarely seen apart. The two of them became entwined like two strands of a cord, twisting together making one stronger piece. The epitome of their affection for one another became permanently evident when they visited Darren's mate in town and had a tattoo each, on their upper arms. Tracey's was on her right and Darren's on his left in order that when the two linked arms the tattoos would touch. 'Trasy heart Darren.' 'Darren heart Trasy.' The names were crudely etched into the flesh in a dark blue script with a red heart between them. Darren's mate was not the most wonderful of artists and not the sharpest knife in the draw, he had spelt Tracey's name with an 'S', and it *hurt!* It would hurt much more in the future but Tracey didn't yet know it. Eventually this relationship had other repercussions as Tracey had become pregnant at the age of fifteen, and again at sixteen. She had remained at home with her parents in the beginning keeping the baby in her own tiny room, but now the little terraced house was too small for another child and Tracey was unceremoniously told to leave. No care was given as to where she would go no fear for her or her baby's future, only for the inconvenience it now caused.

There had been so many ups and downs for her and Darren. Being pregnant again, so young was perhaps a downside although it did mean that the council would now have to provide them with accommodation. It therefore also meant that they could live 'happily ever after' as a family unit, cosy in their little dwelling space, and shut out the rest of the awful world outside.

Rarely though, do fairy tales come true. Reality hit these two naïve young people the minute they were alone in their fairy council castle. Tracey was pregnant with baby number two and Darren had no job, not that this had ever bothered him. He was quite content to sit around all day doing less than nothing. Excitement to Darren was ripping a can of lager from a new pack of six, or inviting his boozy mates in for a game or two of cards, whilst Tracey battled to keep up with their demands for sandwiches or chip butties, struggling to reach the countertop from beyond her growing bulge. The days would usually end with Tracey tired and hungry because what little food she had managed to buy with their benefit was now in the satisfied bellies of Darren and his mates. The baby, Scott, would make attempts at walking because he was largely ignored. This was the only way in which he could keep sight of his mother, though his screams of hunger fell on deaf ears. Tracey would busy herself, cleaning up the mess left behind. The cigarette ends which left little burnt circles on the bare floorboards, the ash which came to rest wherever it fell and the empty cans strewn around the room. She angrily grabbed the plastic holder which once held the lager cans, from Scott's tiny mouth as he attempted to eat it in desperation. The baby inside her leapt, but not with joy. Where was Darren, she thought after all his cronies had gone and the flat fell silent? She waved her way through the cloud of stale tobacco smoke and sure enough her eyes fell upon his prone body on the couch, deep in an unconscious sleep once more.

Tracey didn't clean her castle much after this and she had many good reasons but mainly right now of course, her energies were low. Scott screamed twenty four seven, physically she was so huge she could barely walk, and it just seemed such an endless and pointless task. No one ever walked in and said 'the house looks nice today dear.' There were no visitors other than Darren's mates to appreciate the effort she made in trying to keep everything pristine. She couldn't even understand any more why she had been so enraptured by Darren in the first place. Although he was youthful and experienced to Tracey, he was hardly Brad Pitt! He didn't really have a 'six pack' (other than the ones usually attached to his hand) it was more like an 'off-licence' as his girth was gradually growing due to the regular intake of alcohol. She quietly laughed at the sort of jokey analogy she had just made as she gazed out of her window, bereft of curtains, at the rooftops of the little terraced houses in the streets beyond. Her mind drifted back to her youth growing up in one of those little houses and she realised life had been little better than it was now. What happened to her fairy tale, her dreams? The only one that now popped into her head was Beauty and The Beast, yet she felt she was no longer a beauty and Darren had turned into 'The Beast.'

Her day dreams were shattered by Scott's piercing screams. He was trying to drink the remains of Tracey's glass of water which she had left on the floor beside her chair. But as his tiny fingers tried to grasp the slippery glass, it fell to the bare wooden floor and smashed. The shards of glass bounced back into the air and Scott was peppered with tiny fragments, and his bare little feet were cut as he tried to totter across the room to his astonished mother. Tracey scooped up Scott and ran to the kitchen sink, turned on the tap and unceremoniously drenched Scott's little nappy clad body. She wasn't sure whether it was freezing cold water or searingly hot! It did the job, it washed away the blood as it mingled and curdled down the plughole. Tracey knew she couldn't take Scott to hospital. This would be a case of neglect and she was sure there would be repercussions.

She felt a sharp pain in her abdomen, followed by another. Her labour had begun. Perhaps the shock and fear had brought it on. After comforting Scott and placing him in his cot, she rang for an ambulance and left the flat as she waved a silent goodbye to Darren's sleeping frame. She had dealt with so many things on her own and this would be no exception. By the time she came home, Darren would be a father again, blissfully unaware of the pain and suffering his child's entry into the world would cause for Tracey.

At 4.25 a.m. Jared slithered into the world. This should be a joyous occasion for most mothers, but for Tracey it was anything but. She was beginning to realize that life was just about to get worse. *Now* there was another mouth to feed and another little body to clothe. She was already planning that some of Scott's clothes could be handed down to Jared. She had packed a few things for the baby to wear during her day or two in hospital. As baby Jared slept in his crib, she pulled from her overnight bag, a pack of cheap nappies and a little vest that had once been white. She mused as to how good it was that she'd given birth to a boy, as grey wouldn't have looked so good on a girl. She'd also brought with her the little spotty Babygro worn by Scott when he was tiny, now stained around the poppers with tomato soup which Tracey had given him when there was little else to eat.

Her mind was momentarily brought back to reality with the clanging of heavy doors and the shrill bell that heralded meal time in the prison. Tracey wasn't hungry and asked the warder if she could be allowed to stay in her cell.

"Just this once!" replied the stern – almost male voice of the prison warder, who then left her alone once more.

Tracey mulled over the irony of this situation. She remembered the years of days when there had been virtually nothing to eat, yet now, here she was with a plentiful supply of food which had been prepared for her. She hadn't even needed to open a can or fry a chip and yet she couldn't face putting anything into her aching stomach.

Unhappy as Tracey was, she just wanted to get back to her even unhappier thoughts. Almost as though going through it all in her mind was like reading a book which she could then put away and forget about, perhaps move on to a happier story. But Tracey now knew that her life would *never* be happy, this story would never end, it could never be put down on a shelf, yet it would now be picked up and re-read every single day. She tried desperately to glean anything remotely rosy-tinted from her black memories and remembered the birth of each of her children and that through the physical and mental pain, there had been brief moments of joy when she had looked at their small wrinkled faces as they emerged from her womb, and took their first breath of the black air she felt they would breathe for the rest of their lives. She then sank back into her pillow and even deeper into despair.

The faces of her babies now drifted into her mind's eye. There was Scott; he had big bright blue eyes, like Darren. A year later there had been Jared, he had been harder to care for due to the fact that the family had then moved into their own accommodation and Tracey had received little help from anyone. Then came Libby, ah, little Libby. She had been Tracy's first girl, her princess. Tears fell from her eyes as she recalled how she had so wanted to clothe her princess in pink fluffy dresses and white lacy socks, when all she could give her were Scott and Jared's old Babygros now decorated with tiny holes and yet more tomato soup stains. She'd had no-one to buy her beautiful gifts or send her flowers and chocolates whilst she was propped up on plump pristine pillows, by attentive nurses, she herself looking radiant at the culmination of her pregnancy. She had sat on her bed alone, everyone around her with their families at visiting time, cooing over their newborns, whilst Darren wet the baby's head in the pub with his mates – again, and again. More and more Tracey was assuring herself that she had done the right thing, despite this landing her where she was, as she cried alone.

Tracey wanted to continue her 'mind story' as if she *had* to get to the end in her head to enable her to make sense of it all, as the memories continued to drift. She recalled that little Polly was the next to make an entrance less than a year after Libby. She had been a troublesome birth. Tracey remembered thinking it almost felt as if this baby was holding on to her umbilical cord and was determined not to let go. Stubborn, like her father, and this was how Polly would be, stubborn! Then there was little Beth, sweet little Beth, very different from Polly, quite placid and smiley all of which didn't seem to fit with her grim surroundings. Pop, pop, pop, Tracey thought, like little bullets, her kids had popped out. This had to stop!

The next couple of years had been perhaps the happiest, Tracey recalled in her mind story. Darren had now progressed into a permanent drunken stupor and added a few drugs to his menu. He would sleep most of the day and wake, sort of, by the evening to meet up with his buddies for a drink and drug session somewhere. Some of the children were now attending nursery, largely encouraged by a neighbour, Jenny, who found it so hard listening to the cries of Tracey's children. Jenny had kind of taken Tracey under her very feathery wing, giving her clothes that her own children had out-grown, and toys, something Tracey's children had been bereft of. There had never been any money for toys.

The best thing about Darren's permanent euphoric state meant there was no sex any more, which meant no more kids. Contraception had never occurred to Tracey. There had been no guidance in her young life and quite honestly, in her family, sex was *not* something people wanted to protect themselves from! Therefore there was plenty of it and these poor, unwanted children were the end result.

It brought a little smile to Tracey's tear stained cheeks as she remembered how this was a new lease of life for her. Some of the children at nursery for a couple of hours meant she could stick the younger ones in the pram and go out in the fresh, smog-filled city air for a while. She still wasn't inclined to attempt housework. She would sweep the room with a glance, rather than a vacuum cleaner, as she threw on the red coat Jenny had given her, and shut the door behind her. Occasionally Jenny would baby-sit for her, so that she could take up a part-time job in a bar over the lunch period, bringing in an extra few pounds a week, which Darren knew nothing about. His brain was otherwise occupied and he hadn't even realised his partner was leaving the house every day, or even of the existence of Jenny. He didn't care either, so long as he had his drink, drugs and fags.

To say that Tracey enjoyed her new-found freedom was a gross understatement. She was mixing with people of her own age, who also lived on the estate. People whom she felt had better lives than she did, and she aspired to climb the social ladder herself. This would mean food on the table, curtains to the window and maybe a rug or two on the floor. Best of all, she could save a pound or two each week and occasionally buy herself a new T shirt to wear when working behind the bar or a new pair of three inch heeled fakeskin snakeskin shoes. She had a neat little figure despite bearing so many children and her new life also caused Tracey's lips to turn upwards in a smile occasionally, rather than downwards in sadness. This drew a great deal of male attention which Tracy naturally lapped up. Darren had been the only boy for her, she hadn't previously had the time or opportunity to notice other boys or men, and she was quite enjoying the experience. There was one young man in particular who would pop in every day on his lunch break from the big store across the road, have a pint and a sandwich, a chat with Tracy when she wasn't busy, and back to his job over the road, as store manager. His name was Max. He was an amiable young man, quite ambitious; he had worked his way through various positions at the store over the years, from the stock room to sales assistant, to Manager. Tracey saw something in Max that she had never seen in Darren, not least that he worked very hard and sometimes long hours. She hadn't paid a great deal of attention at first because he wasn't as handsome as Darren had appeared to be in the beginning, yet he had what Darren lacked – a personality! He was caring and interesting to talk to.

Inevitably they became closer and in his old –fashioned and charming manner, Max asked Tracey out on a date. He didn't know about Darren or that she was married. Tracey had found it conveniently easy to leave him out of the equation in her conversations with Max, and she had *always* made certain that the tattoo on her right upper arm bearing the fact that Tracey had once 'heart' Darren, was covered at all times, no matter how warm the weather had been.

Max arranged a date with Tracey and he offered to pick her up from home in his shiny red sports car. Tracey was horrified! The beautiful car and the lovely Max would not feel comfortable waiting outside the flats on the council estate. The local kids would wreck it in seconds and the aroma of cannabis and the neighbours twitching curtains would deter him from returning ever again. No! Therefore she thought up some convincing excuse and they agreed to meet at a small pub on the outskirts of town and Tracey could take the bus. No fear of Jenny or any other nosey neighbours 'advising' her of what she should do. She and Jenny were no longer friends. The level of neglect in the home and around the children had reached a point where Jenny had had great concerns and found herself calling Social Services. This had ultimately resulted in all of the children being taken into care. Darren barely noticed except that the peace and quiet was a bonus to him. Tracey was understandably upset, she had struggled alone for a long time, but her newfound freedom obliterated all thoughts of her old life. She felt her kids would be o.k. wherever they were, and had quickly come to terms with it, for now.

The bus was late, and she was panicking that Max wouldn't wait for her. She wasn't accustomed to any leniency in her life and couldn't imagine why anyone would wait for her. But Max *did* wait. He was becoming increasingly fond of Tracey. He knew nothing about her or her life, just what he saw each day at the bar. He saw no signs of children, Tracey had kept her figure. He didn't see the council estate in her he saw a nicely dressed, pleasantly mannered attractive woman, whom he had come to like, a lot.

'He's there!' lovely reliable Max was there, sitting in his little red sports car, and he was dressed in a *suit*! Tracey had never been out with anyone in a suit before. She climbed into the only other seat in the vehicle, next to Max. The aromas filled her senses, the scent of his aftershave mingling with the smell of the leather covering the seats and the dashboard, the smell of fuel as he revved the engine. Her ears met the roar as they sped off to the hotel that Max had chosen for dinner.

Tracey really looked the part. She had bought herself a close-fitting red dress and in the red car she felt she had blended, become a part of it like a fixed limb, sensuously synchronised as it moved elegantly through the streets. She let her hair loose and felt the breeze breathe on her from the open roof and tousle the wisps of hair around her face as though he was saying 'What are you doing?' She didn't care, she was on a high which no drug could ever induce. No, this was the euphoric effect of happiness, a completely unidentifiable emotion for Tracey.

It was a wonderful evening which had culminated in the two of them staying the night in the hotel. If Tracey had known the right word she would have chosen enchantment, but because she wasn't good with words she couldn't think of a posh one, and therefore just languished in the feeling she was experiencing. As morning approached, Max and Tracey dressed and gathered their belongings, Max paid the bill with his Gold card and the two of them kissed as they sauntered out to the car park with heavy hearts. They had enjoyed each other's company and been so enraptured that they wanted to shut out the rest of the entire world and not have to return to the daily grind of life itself.

As they stepped outside and approached Max's car, the euphoric feeling turned to one of sheer horror. Acid had been thrown over the shiny red paint which was now crumpling and peeling and sizzling. Who could, or would have done this? Max was reeling. The pride and joy that he had worked so hard for was virtually dissolving before his eyes. In blind panic both Max and Tracey were spinning around, seeking anybody or anything which might give them some clue. Max could see nothing, just one or two other vehicles in the car park. Tracey on the other hand froze! There was a white Ford van a few yards away, and Darren was standing beside it. It seems a mate who frequents the bar where Tracey works, had tipped him off, and here was his revenge, or could it be Tracey's punishment? Immediately, Tracey felt she deserved it. Her usual self-deprecating persona returned to her like a slap in the face. She had been unfaithful to Darren, there was no doubt about that, but poor Max, he had done nothing. He *knew* nothing about the relationship Tracey had endured all these years and was perplexed at what was now unfolding before him, in the quiet early morning light.

When total realisation had awoken in Tracey she immediately approached Darren, begging him to just go home, quickly, before the police were called. But Darren was oblivious to Tracey's pleas, his mind was in another place provided courtesy of whichever drugs he had taken that day. He brushed her aside with a strength he didn't realise and she fell to the gravel. As she lay there sobbing, she saw the morning sun glint on the blade of the knife Darren was clutching in his hand, and the familiar horror struck once more.

It was too late. In the seconds it took Tracey to prize her knees out of the sharp gravel driveway, Darren had plunged the blade into Max's chest, he hadn't even had time to see it coming his way. As he was slowly falling to the ground, the last thing Max would see was Tracey's desperate face. The smile he had always been so accustomed to, had dissolved, this was not *his* Tracey who stood before him, fading with each second of what was left of his life.

As life itself was ebbing away from Max, shock dominated Tracey and altered her mind state. Perhaps the body's defences, as though by changing the thoughts to trivia it somehow enables the body to cope with unimaginable events. She watched in awe as the blood oozed from beneath Max's body and swirled around the wheels of his once, shiny red car and marvelled at how well his blood matched the colour.

Reality now boomed back into Tracey's brain. She turned to see Max's executioner standing satisfied and gloating as he grinned at the scene before him. The wrecked car that *he* could never own, the life before him that was now lying dead on the ground, the ultimate betrayal was avenged. He had won, and that was important to Darren.

Tracey's eyes fell upon the dripping blade held loosely in Darren's blood-stained hand and in a moment of anger and complete devastation, she lunged at him, grabbing the sharp naked blade in her equally naked hand, she pulled It from Darren's grasp, twirled it almost expertly, and plunged it into Darren's body again and again and again. Ten times the knife seared through his flesh to the hilt. Still, there was no-one around at this early hour. No-one to stop the horror unfolding, other than Darren's mate in the white van who drove out of that car park like a bat out of hell, with wheels squealing as he fled.

Tracey was now in a blind fury. All the years of control under Darren's rule came flooding back to her and even in those seconds she was making comparisons between this, and the wonderful feeling of self-worth she had received from Max. Darren *had* to suffer. It wasn't enough in that moment that Darren should feel only the physical pain she was inflicting in her fury, there had to be more. As she pulled the knife one last time from Darren's chest her tears mingling with his blood, she rose from her kneeling position astride him and ripped at his T shirt sleeve. There was one last thing left for her to do. She must remove all connection there had ever been between herself and this monster. This animal who had taken from her the only person she had ever *truly* loved. With one last surge of her physical strength, she began to hack furiously at the tattoo on Darren's left arm. Cutting out the canker that lied about "Darren heart Tracey" and then it dawned on her that she herself bore the lie that "Tracey heart Darren."

No more she thought, and as her energy began to ebb she sank to the ground once more and cut away her own tattoo without so much as a murmur. She sat there for what seemed an eternity and ironically laughed internally at the realisation that Max's, Darren's and her own blood, were now merging together as though they would forever be a trinity entwined. The whole sorry affair had unfolded in only minutes to the outside world. The staff at the hotel were now beginning to arrive for their morning shift and were alerted to the noise drifting from the car park. Someone had contacted the emergency services. Darren and Max were strangely placed together in the coroner's vehicle. Darren had claimed her happiness in the form of Max once more, even in death he had taken him from her. Tracey felt a strange envy at this as she herself was taken to hospital, alone.

As she turned the last page of the mind story, her silent horror was broken momentarily by the prison guard entering Tracey's cell, asking if she was o.k. It was in this moment that her mind was now awash with colour – RED! The red car, the red dress, the red coat Jenny had given her, and the deep, gloopy red blood, of this sad, sad trio, blended together. Tracey's mind story had ended, just as she felt her life had too.

She was shortly to discover that she was pregnant yet again. The only glow on the horizon was that this was most certainly Max's child. Either way, what did it matter, the child would have had no father whichever way she looked at it.

CHAPTER SIX

"Sally! I have to go now, Libby's home." Whispered Maria hurriedly.

She rearranged her hair, straightened her blouse and consciously placed a smile on her face as she entered the living room, to greet Libby.

"Romeo and Juliet!" announced Libby with a flourish, as she flung her coat and bag onto Robert's favourite armchair.

After the sad account that Maria had just read through with Sally on the 'phone, she couldn't believe her ears. "What?" Puzzled Maria.

"Romeo and Juliet." Reinforced Libby. "Me and Darren, from the chip shop, are entering the fancy-dress as the star-crossed lovers, with a fateful end." Libby performed, with the back of her hand across her brow and the other one across her heart. Libby had absolutely no idea of the relevance of the analogy she had just made in relation to her parents.

'Wow!' Thought Maria. This was mind blowing and she knew not how she was going to tell Libby the truth. But not today, Libby was in a happy mood and Maria didn't want to spoil it. The village fête was a couple of weeks away and Polly was coming to spend a few days with them she and Sally had agreed to wait at least until after then for a meeting with the girls social workers Grace and Anna.

Events were spiralling out of control and even Maria was beginning to feel a little out of her depth with this one. She did what she always did when she needed to think, and stood out on the balcony with a large glass of wine in her hand, overlooking the little village of Bradwell below. The sun was shining and the weather forecast was good for the fête and the week's activities. Wakes Week, it was called. Maria was sure it must have some religious meaning, something to do with thanking God for the rain. She didn't really care right now; she had other things, other festivities on her mind, those of Libby's eighteenth birthday party. She decided she would speak to Sally face to face when she and John came over for the Gala day. All of the foster carers should sit down together and discuss the enormity of this. Maria was also trying desperately not to allow all of it to scupper the other, secret plans she was making for Libby.

Friday night, and Libby, and Darren from the chip shop were giving the costumes they had made, a test drive before the big day. With a fine white sheet, Libby had created a simple empire line dress, with a drawstring under her bosom. She combed her fine blond hair and placed a plaited band around her forehead. With a little blush and lip gloss and a single bloom from the garden draped across her elbow, she looked for all the world like the beautiful Juliet. Darren had borrowed a pair of his mother's tights. She always wore a heavy denier in order to cover her plump legs, which were ideal for covering Darren's knobbly knees. He struggled clumsily to pull them up without prodding a finger through the nylon hose. Libby had created a simple tabard and a little velvet hat, through which Darren had unceremoniously threaded a loose Magpie feather he had found in the churchyard. It was such fun during Wakes week. The whole village came together at this time. There were the Well Dressings which were veritable works of art with clay and flowers and twigs etc. There was the Brass Band which played its old familiar repertoire as it marched through the main street. The drays which were mostly the cars belonging to the fathers of the various village Gala Queens, would be encrusted with tissue paper roses, in all colours or perhaps a well-known cartoon character would be shaped meticulously. The same old costumes would be paraded by the same old villagers, year after year. Though occasionally someone would create something new and different, which is what Libby and Darren from the chip shop had plotted together.

Libby was so excited on Saturday morning when she woke up. She had taken part in the annual fancy dress parade since she was little. Maria always took such pride in the costume she had put together for her. But this time it was *extra* exciting as Libby had pounced on this idea, *and* made the costumes all by herself. She fussed at her mirror about which colour lip gloss to wear, and whether to pluck a rose, which might be a bit thorny, or a chrysanthemum from the garden.

Maria slowly and pensively began to prepare the food for all her visitors that day. Though the usual zeal eluded her. 'How many have we today?' she thought. 'There's me and Robert, Sally and John, oh and Bruce and Billy, Libby, Polly, Harriet and Fiona are coming home from Uni'. Oh, and Mrs. Harris from the village.' She pondered as she counted on her fingers. 'Mm, at least eleven. I'll cater for a dozen or more to be on the safe side.'

Maria could hear the brass band in the little main street below, tuning up in preparation for their most important performance of the day. She could smell the aroma of the sheep which was already set to roast on the spit on the village green, all day it took. She daydreamed about the fact that at the end of it all one poor sheep could only produce so many lamb sandwiches. They couldn't possibly feed the entire village. 'Who did they think they were? 'She thought to herself. 'Jesus feeding the 5,000?' She then stopped herself and quietly reprimanded her wicked blasphemous thoughts, and sipped her wine, there on the balcony. It was midday, and she could see below in the village, the little paper rose- covered cars making their way to the starting point. The Boy-Scouts were setting up their bring-and-buy stall and the Women's Guild were sticking the little coloured numbered tickets on their Tombola prizes. The podium in the middle of the Green, was having the finishing touches made to the blue velvet drapes, awaiting the presence of the newly appointed 'Queen.' Libby had often wanted to be village Queen, but now, almost in her eighteenth year she had passed beyond all that and simply enjoyed the frivolity and joy of everyone around her.

"Sausage rolls!" Thought Maria. She had put them in the oven before pouring her glass of wine and could now smell their lovely fresh warm 'bakeyness.' She carefully placed them, from the oven onto a cooling rack, and jumped back to reality as Libby swept into the kitchen.

"Ta Da!" She called, standing there with open arms, and quickly did a twirl, flouncing her home-made Juliet dress. Her beautiful blonde hair drifting on the scented breeze she had created.

"Oh *my*, you look amazing!" said Maria with a smile.

"Isn't it great? I'm just going to meet Polly, and Sally and John at the bus stop from the one O'clock bus. See you later." And she ran out of the kitchen. She took a step backwards as she drifted through the hallway to snatch a gladiolus from the vase of flowers Maria had lovingly arranged. 'Just the thing.' She thought. 'Nice and drapey and romantic.' It had lovely peachy hues which stood out against her pale dress.

As she wandered down the lane she called to others who were making their way to the village green for the celebrations. Robert had gone to pick up old Mrs. Harris, who was usually on her own, poor thing and Libby waved as they passed her in the car. Harry Jones from the new houses on the fringe of the village was dressed as Henry Viii.

"Whoa – wicked!" Libby called to him with her thumbs pointing skyward. The Benson twins were dressed as Tweedle Dum and Tweedle Dee. The Fire Brigade were out in full force and full uniform, preparing the engine, polishing the chrome bits and pieces and preparing the hoses with which they would squirt water at bystanders. This was their chance to have a go at anyone who may have upset them, but it was all in good fun.

Darren was waiting at the bus stop on the main street, looking more amusing than romantic and feeling very obviously uncomfortable wearing his mother's tights. Libby joined him and as they waited for the bus, she began straightening his outfit, twisting the feather in his hat and attempting to smooth out the wrinkles in his tights. She chastised him for his gloomy face, and told him he looked more like a petulant child than 'Romeo!' Their relationship was one more like a mother guiding a wayward son, than boyfriend/girlfriend. But as yet Libby had had little opportunity to spread her wings. There was time yet.

CHAPTER SEVEN

"C'mon. Hurry up Poll, we'll miss the bus." Called Sally.

John was putting on a shirt and tie. It was quite an adventure visiting the countryside and he liked to make a good impression.

Polly was donning her favourite pair of jeans. There was no *way* she was putting on any aires and graces. Or rather, that was the impression she liked to give. Secretly though, she quite enjoyed visiting her sister. More to the point she loved the village fete each year. She had come to know people, and the entire village knew Polly, and each time they saw her, they would demonstrate their affection and amazement at how much she had grown. Old Samuel who lived at the top of the lane would stop on the street and rest on his walking stick, look her up and down and say, "Eh lass, tha's grown a fair bit since ah last saw thee." Same old words, but Polly would simply smile and say thank you. Mrs. Roberts who worked in the bakery would call to her and ask how she'd been. The conversation would always end with a free cream bun or a vanilla slice. Billy would place his floral deck-chair on the pavement outside his cottage in preparation for the Parade, in order to get a good view and woe betide anyone who stood in his way! The youngsters would stop for a chat with him and he would naughtily pinch a chip or two from the greasy snacks they had purchased from the chip shop. The very chip shop where Darren's mum sweltered in her thirty denier tights.

The tuning up of the Brass Band could be faintly heard throughout the village. Then suddenly and without warning, the big base drum boomed! "Boom Boom" pause "Boom Boom" and away they all went, marching down the main street, leading the parade. Each instrument could be clearly heard. The trumpets, the trombones, each musician had not only to concentrate on the sheet of music before him or her, but also on the left right left, left right left, of their rhythmic marching feet. All were perfectly attuned in one motion and one sound. They had practised well.

There was somebody, no-one could recognise, dressed as Donald Duck, another as Snow White with members of the village nursery as her seven small friends. The local G.P. Dr. Samson led his usual ragtime band, stepping in tune with them and dipping his large umbrella up and down in time with the music. It's swaying fringing, shimmering in the sunlight. By late afternoon, the Brass Band was silent, the Queen had been crowned, the Tombola stall was empty, and Libby and Darren had won first prize in the fancy dress. Possibly more due to the fact that it was a new entry and not the same old characters as the year

56

before, rather than poor Darren's non-existent romantic smile at his Juliet. The tights had taken their toll! Libby had tried to teach him to bow, with one leg extended, doffing his hat with a twirl of his hand as he dipped and bowed, but it appeared more like an attempt at the splits from Darren and after so much practising, and his tights were now wrinkled to the point that they resembled a pair of elephant's trunks. But everyone had had such a fun time and made their weary way home, leaving the village green strewn with litter, Tombola tickets and ice cream wrappers.

Back at home, Maria, Robert, Sally and John had sat down with a cup of tea to discuss the current situation, whilst all the children were down in the village having fun. Even days after reading the social workers report, the horror of the situation was still only slowly sinking in for all of them. Maria and Sally with their maternal instincts were debating together about the impact on *all* of these siblings not only Libby and Polly. Their hearts went out to all of them though they had little knowledge yet, of their whereabouts.

A decision had to be made as to how and when they should break the news to these kids. It was finally considered best to at least wait until after Libby's eighteenth. The girls had had no contact with any of their birth family, this had been a court ruling, but also some or all of the siblings had been adopted. It wasn't going to be easy.

"Oh come on" said Maria, rising suddenly from her chair. "Let's all go for a walk around the village for a little fresh air."

Sally and John were all for that. They loved the quaintness of everything. It was a stark contrast to their little house with red brick walls. Maria's balcony with its breathtaking view of the valley and the village below, and her wonderful garden with manicured lawns was quite different from their own white plastic table and chairs in the corner of their postage stamp yard.

As they strolled down the lane the sun was shining on the natural thick stone walls of the little cottages. The little old pub on the corner had had a new coat of whitewash and people were relaxing with a pint or two on the wooden benches outside. The schoolyard was silent; all of the children were doing other things today. Sally had little silent thoughts to herself as though her brain was trying so hard to shut other things out completely. How strange it is that the weeds grow so quickly between the paving stones of the school driveway when little feet are not trampling on them each day. How silent the church graveyard was, despite there being so many people around, living, and dead. There was almost an air of reverence cast over the gravestones like a fishing net, though it annoyed Sally greatly how the jackdaws and magpies held no reverence or dignity at all with their incessant squawking. She remembered the expression 'Waking the Dead' and thought these must be Satan's sentinels, their duty to ensure the dead couldn't rest in peace, neither could her thoughts, and the noise brought her back to reality.

"Look at the Well Dressing" mused Maria.

Sally read out this year's chosen text describing the scene, depicted in flower petals and other natural materials.

'The Return of the Dove' Genesis chapter 8 verse eleven, she read. The picture was that of Noah standing on the bow of the Ark with arms outstretched before him, and in the blue sky crafted from the petals of blue rhododendrons was a dove just as expertly crafted from the finest sheep's wool bearing an olive branch in its beak.

"How lovely." Sally softly whispered.

Maria on the other hand was creating allegories with everything in her mind. "Huh! How ironic" she thought. "Lucky Noah, he managed to save *his* family. How on earth are we going to save ours from the heartache which was to come?" And as she rolled her head backwards her eyes rested upon the church tower, with its spire reaching skywards. 'The Finger of God!' pointing upwards to his abode. Rather like a road sign saying 'This way to salvation!' Was this a reminder to Maria that she should perhaps ask Him for help? She not only needed help with the present situation, but the secret project she had begun, now had a new slant on it.

The little group moved slowly into the church, their demeanour like that of a congregation of mourners at a funeral. 'This should be a happy day' thought Maria and she put all these sad things to the back of her mind and began her little commentary to the others, with opinions on the crafts of local villagers exhibited along the pews of the church. She glanced quickly and fleetingly at the effigy of Christ on the cross. Something Maria was not greatly fond of and now it was all the more poignant as her eyes fell on the blood flowing from Christ's hands and feet. 'Strange isn't it' she thought, 'how otherwise it might be barely noticed, yet with the present situation it somehow bore a greater significance.

The mood was lifted somewhat as they mingled and marvelled at the beauty of the wood carvings and the embroidery that was on display. It was then time for a cup of tea and a cake in the village school rooms, prepared lovingly by the ladies of the Women's Guild. There were cupcakes in various pastel hues, sitting proudly on the glass cake stand. A carrot cake adorned with little marzipan carrots, chocolate fudge cake dripping with glossy chocolate sauce. The floppy little paper plates could barely hold the sizes of the wedges placed upon them as they were sliced and served to those who could barely wait, salivating as the flavours melted on their tongue, their eyes closing to prolong the sensation of bliss. The mood was even further lifted as Polly and Libby came giggling toward their pseudo-parents respectively, asking for money to buy a big squishy piece of tempting chocolate cake.

"Maria, I won a bottle of wine on the Tombola. Mrs. Brown let me have it on the promise that I would bring it straight to you, and that I would have it on my eighteenth birthday, so here, you have to save it for me."

The sentence came out like a train out of a tunnel and left Libby breathless with happiness and laughter. Polly was equally exuberant. She had won a large cuddly toy rabbit which was definitely more up her street. Polly wasn't into the party scene, she was more of a tomboy and usually much happier at the Hollywood Bowl in town, or the new Ice Rink, speeding round, her skates making a slicing sound as she swept past the other skaters, timing herself, constantly trying to beat her own record as though it would bring great satisfaction to compete even against herself.

However, everyone had enjoyed the day. Sally popped into the playing field on their weary way up the hill, to call Bruce and Billy, who had spent much of the day on the swings and roundabout, or playing football on the vast field with some of the boys from the village. As the little troupe climbed the hill, the church clock chimed 'ding dong', 'ding dong', followed by five 'dongs'. The finger of God was saying 'Go home!'

It was now time for Maria to shine at what she did best. Dinner parties! Though this wasn't as grand as those she would usually display for her or Robert's colleagues on occasions. Sally and John were very down to earth sort of people. As Sally herself would say fondly "We're just a couple of 'Townies', you don't need to impress us." Maria knew this and actually enjoyed the fact that, although she couldn't bare it if the plates and the napkins didn't match, she could to some degree relax with this family. She didn't have to serve the food to them, they were happy enough to wander into the kitchen and help themselves to what was there. Maria's daughters Harriet and Fiona found it fondly amusing. They had grown used to feeding themselves, humbled as students, and found their mother's fussing tedious and unnecessary. This therefore was a refreshing change, to see her relaxed and un-phased by this chaotic food fest in her kitchen. Maria had cooked good plain old beef stew and dumplings with soft fresh granary bread from the bakery. She had baked the lovely sausage rolls, to follow, which she'd had to hide from the family, and a rich Dundee cake which was set down on the table with best butter, deliciously waiting in her Spode butter dish. She knew John loved to spread butter thickly on his Dundee cake.

These two families, entwined and joined by the love they had for their foster daughters, now sat having pleasant conversation well into the evening, when Robert very kindly offered to take the family back to Sheffield as they had missed the last bus, and taxis were not an easy option in the countryside. Billy and Bruce slept the whole way home in the back of Robert's M.P.V. Polly had thoughts jangling in her head. She had enjoyed her day so much, and a little envy of Libby fleetingly fluttered into her head. She secretly wished she lived in this cosy friendly little village cosseted by neighbourly affection. It was almost like 'group parenting', where the whole village ensured Libby was cared for and nurtured, they advised her constantly and always took great collective interest in her welfare. But this thought soon passed as Polly realised her injustice to Sally and John. They were wonderful foster parents, like *real* parents to her. Sally's motherly ways were comforting, as she would take Polly's face between her chubby hands and plant a whopping soppy kiss on her brow. Polly would squirm and frown, and wipe away the invisible saliva with a sweep of the back of her hand. This was a protest Sally was familiar with, yet she knew deep down thatPolly appreciated it yet there was no way she could let her guard down. Polly wasn't about to let anyone into her thoughts. She didn't have the ability her sister had, to lock them all away in a Pandora's Box and throw away the key. No, Polly's thoughts were with her daily. She felt this was what gave her a more cynical outlook on life. Whether that is present, or past. The past wouldn't leave her, and she could not let go. The memories were big, and real. Her social worker, Anna Faraday, had often suggested to Polly that they sit down and begin some sort of Life Story project, and perhaps a family tree, but Polly was always reluctant. This would mean facing her demons, the need to question her past and her memories, even to ask about her birth family members and their whereabouts, something which neither of the girls had shown any desire to do.

As the weeks passed, autumn began showing her colours. She clothed the trees in russet and yellow and cast greyish hues across the once blue sky. The low sun reflected like gold on the windows of the college as Polly walked along its tree lined avenue. The leaves were falling, slowly fluttering to the ground like discarded children as though their umbilical cord of life had been cut off from the mother tree. Dry, and spent like little skeletons as they crunched beneath her feet. This was a deceased family tree, rather like her own may be, if she dug up the truth. How Polly wished at that moment that she could think like her sister. Libby wouldn't see this act of nature as she did. No, Libby in all probability would see the leaves as dancing fairies in their gold and bronze gowns, creating some sort of magic carpet for Princess Libby to walk on. Polly stopped herself. Poor Libby, she was denying reality, shutting it out with her airy-fairy thoughts and one day it would all catch up with her – with both of them. Anyhow, Polly thrust her head backwards, and deeply breathed in the sharp frosty air like medication. Clearing her mind for the day ahead on her new course in Health and Social Care, hoping the prescription of fresh frosty air would last the day.

Libby was also preparing herself for Uni'. She looked out of the window and wondered whether or not she should wear a jacket today. She had put it off for as long as possible, she never wanted summer to end, but the frost on the lawn helped her with her decision. She wished she had time to watch the wild rabbits as they hopped around, leaving little thawed patches in the white frosty grass where their warm bodies had sat, and their tiny feet had hopped. The morning bus to town was due, and she mustn't miss it today as Maria had left early this morning and was unable therefore to give her a lift. How she wished she could drive and had a car of her own, it would be so much easier. She held her toast between her teeth as she slid her arms into her coat sleeves and grabbed her bag, almost forgetting to lock the door behind her as she left. Responsibility was something she must take more seriously now that she was almost an adult. A dark thought flickered in her mind, lit only by the candles she remembered along the windowsill, where her father lay beneath on the couch. The panic she had felt back then, resurfaced as she remembered Darren's flailing arm knocking over two of them and the cushion catching fire, rudely waking him. He had then slapped Scott, blaming him for this 'attack' by a candle! Never had Darren been for one moment to blame for the lack of electricity due to his idle lifestyle.

"Flick the switch!" thought Libby, no electricity needed. She appeared to find it relatively easy to switch off these thoughts whenever they crept in, self-preservation perhaps?

The bus trundled its weary way up the hillside and over the moors. It passed the old familiar rock formations on its journey. The Scotsman's Pack, the Toad's Mouth. Romantic notions she thought, but Libby liked that. The sheep never differed; they continually ate grass and wandered the moorland.

'What a life' she thought. Free from all responsibility other than that of eating, and staying alive.

The journey changed as the roads straightened out somewhat. There was the noise of traffic now which woke her from her thoughts. She noticed the bustle of the city, the dirty red brick of the old Victorian houses with their now redundant chimney pots, a remnant of the age before smokeless fuel and central heating.

The bus arrived in the city centre and Libby wearily stepped off, onto the pavements of Sheffield and joined the droves of other students heading for the university, to knuckle down to obtaining her degree.

CHAPTER EIGHT

Maria had left for the office early again today. She had some paperwork to do, for her secret project to deal with before the day began, and then some 'phone calls to make.

"Hello, is that Grace Marsden?" Enquired Maria, receiver in hand.

"Yes, Hi Maria, how are you? I guess you're ringing to ask if I've made further progress with our project.

"Yes that's right" said Maria, relieved that Grace was prepared for her call, and hopeful that she had some new information for her. Indeed Grace had been busy, she was a good social worker compared to some, on the ball and always followed through with agreements. However, she had never done anything like this before and wasn't quite sure just how it was going to work out.

"Well, I've been looking through the records Maria and it would appear that we have three siblings to contact. With Libby and Polly that makes five of them. Then of course there will be the new baby when it's born, a boy I think is expected." Maria stayed quiet, she was taking notes. "So then, to recap, there's Scott, the eldest who's twenty years old who was adopted, now independent. Then there's Jared nineteen also adopted, and of course Libby and Polly. Then there seemed to be a bit of a gap before Beth now almost twelve who is also adopted. The older ones should pose little or no problem once traced, of course Beth is still a minor, and of course, as I said, the new baby, we have our work cut out Maria, but let's give it our best shot!"

Maria was so relieved that Grace was on her side. Her professional yet caring approach had won the day. Working together, the two women would now have a better chance of pulling off what they hoped to achieve. Maria sat down and began writing down her plans.

"O.k. well, with my legal background I would be better suited to tracking down Scott and Jared as they are adults, and perhaps Grace, you could work on Beth and the yet unborn baby, as they are still technically in the care system." Maria's thoughts were racing. She sat back in her big leather chair and placed her fountain pen neatly in the centre of the pages of her notebook. She touched the tips of her fingers to form an arch, which somehow aided her thinking as she swayed gently from side to side, swivelling her executive, leather chair. There was still much planning to do but Maria realised only too well that the plans had to be separated into two categories. Those in which Libby could be involved, and those she must know nothing about. She had to be sensitive. She and Sally had realised that memories were returning to the girls, memories which had been deeply rooted in the core of their very beings, which were beginning to surface. Libby's Pandora's Box was being prized open by the double-edged sword of adulthood. It had stirred in her a different kind of emotion.

On the one hand growing up was great, exciting, doing what she wanted starting Uni' starting the rest of her life! Yet on the other hand it was quite scary. It brought responsibilities and a kind of loneliness she could only relate to her early life. She remembered once more how life had been. How her parents had not shown her or her siblings affection, and when they'd had enough of their children, they were all removed and distributed who knows where. Libby couldn't eject the thought from her head that when she was eighteen perhaps Maria and Robert may have had enough. Maybe they would want a younger child. Where would she be then? She knew she should possess the life-skills and the ability to take care of herself, yet there was still the little child inside her who felt very vulnerable indeed. She hadn't even wanted to live in the Halls of Residence, as her home and family meant so much to her. She was confused. Her airy-fairy ways, were beginning to morph into dark moods and she failed to see how she could prevent them. Would she be cast aside yet again?

Polly was also affected by similar notions yet felt she'd had more of a reprieve than Libby had. She had another year or more to go before *her* milestone. She felt angry at the system. Angry that, although she loved Sally more than the birth mother she could now vaguely remember, she knew that technically she could be made to move at any time. This insecurity was constantly with her, almost like a test of Sally's devotion. Polly reflected on how birthdays should be such fun and happy times, yet each one brought her nearer to that dreaded time when she may have to leave Sally and John's home, and the security of the care system. She felt Libby would be staying with Maria and Robert, but she doubted that Sally and John would be able to afford to keep *her* beyond eighteen. She too was confused. Yet both girls kept their fears and insecurities to themselves.

It was almost 6p.m. and Maria had prepared, as always, a wonderful meal for the family. She knew that Libby would be home any minute on the 5.15 p.m. bus from Sheffield and she wanted to hear all about her experiences at Uni' and looked forward to sitting down for a good hot meal, and perhaps a glass of wine, and a great opportunity for conversation. At ten minutes past six, Libby blustered through the door.

"Hi sweetheart!" Called Maria as she dished up the roast potatoes on the huge serving dish which now held a sizzling beef roast in its centre. "How's your day been?

"Oh, o.k." Replied Libby with an air of despondency. "I made a new friend today. He's called Todd. I really like him, I think we'll be good mates."

"So why so glum then?"

"Oh, nothing, just the time of year. I think I must suffer from that S.A.D. thingy, whatever it is."

"You mean Seasonal Affective Disorder," smiled Maria. "Well it is quite possible love. After all winter's on its way and it makes us all a bit glum, with early dark nights facing us. Hey let's not be so down. We have lots of plans to make. Guess what, I've booked a venue for your party, at the Moon and Stars, on the main road to Hathersage. Oh, Libby, the room is beautiful; all the chairs are gilt framed with red velvet seats. All the tables are big round ones which I think are best for communication, don't you?"

Libby perked up slightly at the notion that her party arrangements were underway. Maria continued to explain about the D.J. who was the son of one of Robert's work colleagues, but 'he was very good!'

"We need to decide what food we would like, and what to drink, oh and of course how many are to be catered for." Maria secretly made a mental note to herself that she would need to add another three to the final list. "Don't forget we need to shop for new clothes Libby. Perhaps I could meet you in town one evening after Uni'. We could trot off to Meadowhall Shopping Centre, plenty of choice there."

Libby had been taught at Maria's hand to enjoy all the exclusive shops, which she loved, yet she also knew there was a great choice of accessories in the cheaper high street stores. She couldn't wait!

The ideas now in Libby's head were so many they were jostling for position at the forefront. The dress, the

earrings, shoes and bag. Should she wear a tiara? Princess Libby? This was more like the Libby Maria knew and they tucked into the sumptuous meal she had prepared.
Robert had arrived home, and Libby wanted to tell them about her new acquaintance, Todd.

"He's twenty years old, a *bit* older than me, he's really good looking, but more than that Maria, we get on so well together."

"I'm so pleased love. It's good to know you're making friends, university can be quite lonely in a crowd otherwise."

Libby *thought* she understood what Maria meant by this, but all she could think of at the moment were the feelings she had for Todd, feelings she hadn't experienced before, yet these emotions had a strange familiarity which Libby could not identify. Todd *was* indeed a handsome young man. The only imperfection which marred his chiselled features, were the tiny scars which peppered his left cheek and forehead. An accident when he was a child apparently. But it was Todd's personality which reached Libby's heart. She felt it actually beat differently, as though little butterflies were touching its mechanism and altering its rhythm. She loved being with him and had to concentrate extra hard during lessons, otherwise she was consumed with the desire for the hands on the clock to race round to lunch, so that she and Todd could eat and talk together. She was now looking forward to her party more than ever and she could barely wait to tell Polly

72

about her new acquaintance. Polly however, was quite unimpressed by the notion of a 'boyfriend.' She wasn't ready for 'that kind of thing yet.' This was something she was *not* envious of and completely uninterested but agreed to meet up with Libby on Saturday in order to be formerly introduced to the wonderful Todd!

Saturday morning, and Libby stepped out of the shower, flung on her bath robe and wrapped her long wet, blond hair in a towel. She was meeting Todd today, *and* Polly. She wanted to look her best, to show off Todd to Polly rather like an accessory, but she also wanted to invite him to her eighteenth birthday party, he would be her guest of honour, he would have the first dance with her. Her dreams were only broken when the hairbrush became entangled in her wet hair as she sat at her dressing table mirror, prepared to style it in a new fashion for a change. The sharp tug on her scalp brought feelings of anger which could only be explained by the memory it brought. The memory of Darren tugging at her fine little curls as a child, screaming his abuse at the presence of head lice! 'Nits' he had called them. She felt shame at this memory, shame at the names Darren had called her for catching 'these filthy things.' He hadn't realised or perhaps accepted the fact that the squalor in which they lived may have been appealing to these little creatures who had found a perfect home in Libby's curly hair. Whatever the cause, Darren had the solution. In anger and haste, he snatched the scissors from the kitchen drawer, and dragged Libby by her nit infested hair, before pulling and cutting until every lock of her infantile femininity was chopped from her head. He had ignored her screams, her fear at the sight of the scissors and what he might do with them. The rest of this dysfunctional family had looked on in silent horror, and fear. Even Tracey had been of little comfort or sanctuary to her brood, overridden by her own fear of Darren. Libby had sobbed in a corner for hours and couldn't even eat what little was offered that night.

As she gazed at her reflection in the mirror, Libby's senses returned to reality and the present. She took refuge in her now flowing locks and had vowed long ago that no-one would cut them ever again without her permission, and proceeded to blow dry her natural curls into an acceptable style. She applied makeup and put on her favourite pair of jeans and top and skipped down the stairs to make arrangements to meet up with Maria later to shop for a party dress.

Polly was already sitting at a table by the window in the coffee shop when Libby arrived, waving across the adjacent coffee drinkers.

"I'll have a Double Caramel frappuccino please." Giggled Libby. Her Pandora's Box had closed its lid for a while and she was in happy mood. Why wouldn't she be, she was meeting Todd, followed by a shopping trip for *THE* dress!

"Oh Poll, he's here!"

Polly looked up from her coffee, and hadn't realised that the creamy foam, sprinkled with cinnamon, was now attached to her upper lip, resembling a gingery moustache. Todd, in true gentlemanly manner, extended his hand in a gesture of greeting towards Polly immediately, and verbalised his greeting accompanied by a wry smile. Polly was not impressed to begin with and felt that Todd was making fun of her in some way. This was Polly's usual self-doubt emerging. She hadn't realised that Todd was desperately trying to conceal his amusement of the foreign body now adorning Polly's upper lip. What he found more amusing and enchanting was the fact that Polly was completely unaware of it.

"Oh look at *you*!" exclaimed Libby "Here let me help you." And she proceeded to wipe Polly's mouth with a paper napkin, much like a doting mother would to her child. Polly was a little embarrassed and gave a shy smile with bowed head. She wasn't accustomed to 'being' around boys and didn't really know what to do or say, but she bluffed her way through in true Polly style.

As the afternoon passed in a haze of chatter and laughter, Polly began to warm to Todd. She wasn't quite sure just *what* her feelings were really. She didn't fancy Todd at all, like in a 'boyfriend' sort of way, but she knew she liked his company and felt somehow akin to him. She was pleased with Libby's choice and hoped they would remain together. She decided she would really like to keep Todd in her life. Before the three parted, Libby approached Todd about her party,

"It's going to be on the first of December at the..."

Todd raised his hands in an effort to stop Libby going any further. His heart was already heavy, but he broke the news that it was impossible for him to attend, due to a prior engagement. "Well can't you make some excuse?" pleaded Libby. "This is really important to me Todd."

"I'm so sorry Libby" he protested. "I know how important it is to you, and under any other circumstances, I wouldn't miss it for the world. But I have to do something which could be life-changing for me, something that cannot be altered or cancelled, I'm really so sorry."

Libby felt hurt. Todd had revealed very little about his life, except that he lived alone in a flat in a suburb of Sheffield. His family apparently didn't live too far away and he saw them frequently, but much of his life he had kept a closely guarded secret. Libby understood this, she too didn't reveal her personal circumstances to those she didn't know too well. As though there was felt to be some shame attached and yet she had *nothing* to feel ashamed about, where Maria and Robert were concerned. They had given her the best life ever! Though she had omitted to mention to Todd that she was in foster care.

"Tell you what Libb'" smiled Todd, "Why don't we fix up another evening, where you, me and Polly could go for a meal together, to celebrate your birthday."

Once again Libby felt a tinge of hurt that he didn't want to take her for a romantic meal, just the two of them, like a fairy tale. Yet at the same time she strangely, didn't feel at

76

all jealous that Polly would be there. She quietly agreed that 'that would be nice.

CHAPTER NINE

Autumn had now finished shedding her leafy family. Dispersing them over a vast area, as the wind blew them afar just like Libby's own family. It was a sad feeling and she wondered whether her mum and dad ever thought of her, of where she had been blown to, on the wind of time. She also thought of her bothers and sister as she stood and gazed at the little skeleton leaves now trodden and squished into the damp earth, their umbilical cords now detached, cut from the mother trees by the cruel wind once more. She watched as Robert raked the huge lawn, rounding up the leaf children, and setting light to the heap in the corner of the garden by the apple tree, effectively cremating them. 'Ashes to ashes, dust to dust, from dust you came and to dust you shall return.' She remembered the vicar quoting that in church somewhere in the past, and now the little leaf children were returning to the dust from whence they came. The apple tree was also shedding her children and the once rosy perfect fruits of her womb were now decaying on the ground. Even they had been unwanted, as Maria hadn't had time lately to bake them into a delicious pie, and yet a few had clung on to the very last. Libby cheered herself at the thought that, the reason for this had been that Maria's time had been taken, making arrangements for *her* party. This made her feel important, wanted, maybe she had truly escaped becoming a 'leaf' child. Libby couldn't make sense of why she felt so sad, deep inside, when here she had so much to look forward to.

"It *must* be that S.A.D. thingy. There's no other reason I can think of to feel this way" she thought. It was Sunday morning. Robert always tidied the garden on a Sunday morning. Today it all seemed so futile to Libby as she stood on the balcony and watched. Though he had caught most of the stray leaf skeletons, more were falling behind him, there were so many. Would he ever be free of them she wondered.

Foster children are like that. There are so many of them scattered around, and never enough places for them to go. 'That's what will happen to me soon, no-one will want me, and they all believe I'm grown up but I'm NOT!' She screamed internally. 'I'm still a little girl inside and I need Maria and Robert, or perhaps I could live with my mum and dad now. Maybe they've changed. They must have missed me; they'd be so pleased to see me, now I'm grown up.'

These thoughts were flying around in Libby's head like the jackdaws in the churchyard with their loud incessant voices. She had noticed Maria being very secretive on occasions recently, and she felt perhaps she and Robert were making plans for her to move on, and be replaced by a younger child. After all they didn't wish to foster 'adults', which technically Libby now was. They took her in when she was a small girl, perhaps *that* was what theyreally wanted, another small girl. Tomorrow was the

79

day of her final L.A.C. review; perhaps she might get some answers then. The L.A.C. (looked after children) review, is a process which takes place every six months, its purpose being to monitor a young person's progress, to record achievements, discuss the placement itself and of course, any areas of concern. Libby was convinced there would be 'areas of concern' tomorrow. Could she sit through this and hear the worst? There would be people from the education department, her social worker Grace Marsden, Maria and the reviewing officer, who would perhaps deliver the bad news. She felt at that moment betrayed by Maria. Why hadn't she given her any clues before now? For Libby this was one occasion where *she* envied Polly. Living in the big city, Polly had places to go. She could disappear just like Libby wanted to do right now, but where would she go in this little village. Anyone she turned to would smile and say "There, there Libby, don't be silly now, go on home." There was no escape. Also, Polly had at least another year before *she* became an adult, another year to be protected and loved by Sally and John. Envy was now being released into Libby's atmosphere; she must close the Pandora's Box before anything else became tainted by these thoughts and fears which were sneaking out of the half closed lid.

"O.k., yes that's great, oh! Must go now, speak to you soon, Bye." Maria ended her 'phone call abruptly as Libby entered the room.

There she goes again, being secretive. Who on earth could she be ringing on a Sunday morning?

"Are you o.k. love? Asked Maria at the sight of such a glum face.

"Yeah, I'm o.k. just a headache." Lied Libby. "Is it o.k. for me to ring Poll for a chat?"

"Of course it is, I'll put the roast in the oven, by the time you two finish it'll be cooked." Joked Maria. But Libby just gave a weak smile and strolled to the lounge for the 'phone.

"Hi Poll, it's only me"

"Oh, Hi, who else would it be?" she laughed. "How's Todd?" enquired Polly.

"Dunno, haven't heard from him today yet. Actually I'm a bit miffed that he isn't coming to my party Poll. I really thought we were getting to know each other well, and I did think I would have been more important than whatever it is he's doing that night, but he's quite secretive at times."

"Give him time, poor fella! No funny business yet then?"

"Polly McIntyre, what *do* you mean? Smiled Libby, and her mood lifted a little as she chatted to her sister. She didn't reveal any more to Polly as to how she was feeling about home, or about Todd. There *was* no 'funny business' between them, Libby hadn't given that a thought and Todd certainly hadn't made any moves, unwanted or otherwise. She really did feel that they would be no more than good friends, perhaps very good friends, and she knew that Polly liked him too, perhaps *they* would develop a relationship, given time.

"Come and get it!" called Maria from the kitchen. Libby said her goodbyes to Polly and sauntered into Maria's space as she was placing the roasting dish in the centre of the table. The joint of meat was sizzling in its juices; the comfy aroma pervaded Libby's senses and diffused her negative feelings ever so slightly. This smell of comfort and love was more evocative than any erotic perfume. As she sat down with the family to a sumptuous Sunday lunch and subdued chatter moved around the meal table, Libby's negative thoughts dissipated into the air like the steam from the sprouts.

CHAPTER TEN

Tracey lay upon her thin prison bed. As she gazed around her, the words of the Tom Jones song came into her head, "As I look around me, at these four grey walls that surround me!"

"Why on earth do they actually paint them *grey?*" she thought, "Perhaps it's an extra punishment for the hapless inmates. What was the song called? "she asked herself silently. "Oh yes, that's it, The Green, Green Grass of Home."

Tracey had never had any green, green grass at *her* home, just the red brick terraced houses and the pavements outside. She allowed her mind to wander, closed her eyes and imagined she was walking through endless fields with the cool softness of the grass beneath her bare feet, the sun beating down on her face, playing hide and seek with her children. Ah! Her children. Where were they all now, she thought. What do they look like, would she recognise them if she passed them in the street, would she ever get to walk down a street again? She didn't even have a photo' of *any* of them to put on her cell wall, like other inmates did. She and Darren couldn't even afford a camera and taking pictures had not been a priority, so there were *none*.

These longings were abruptly cut off by the sharp and sudden abdominal pain which now consumed Tracey's very being. It was thankfully very familiar to her. She had given birth five times before, but this time was different. Her baby would be born, and live it's first few short weeks of life at least, behind prison walls. There had been little discussion with regard to what would happen after that period. But Tracey knew her baby would either be adopted or at the very least have to go into foster care until she had completed her sentence – which could be a long time! It all seemed so futile, this would be her sixth child – and yet she had none of them. 'Bang' another contraction seared through her body like a bullet passing through it. She called the warder and was unceremoniously hauled off to the prison hospital wing. A doctor and a midwife were sent for, and Tracey's labour continued, long and hard into the night.

At 7 a.m. the next morning, the new baby McIntyre slithered into his new cold grey world. His future already uncertain even before he drew his first breath of this closeted air. The cord was cut and he was swaddled in a blanket and returned to Tracey to her waiting arms. He had barely cried as he emerged into the world. How long would it be, she wondered, before he'd scream like the others had? But then she remembered where she was, and if nothing else, food was regular, and there were no Bills to pay. Wow! Some benefits then from being incarcerated. Tracey felt so alone. She'd had no-one to hold her hand or mop her brow, through the birth of any of her children, yet how she missed that. No encouraging words, to push! No hug from her husband or a well deserved 'Well done.' She thought of Max. *He* would have been there, he would have done all these things and been a proud father unlike Darren. The only pleasure in the birth of his children had been the cigar and a pint his mates had bought him down the pub. *He* received the pat on the back and the 'well done.' How misplaced.

Tracey had her own social worker, Mary and especially now that she had a baby to care for, the visits became more regular. She brought bits and pieces for Tracey, one or two luxuries and clothes and blankets for the baby. Also she worked tirelessly to secure the baby's placement with Tracey for as long as they would allow. Mary knew only too well the bonding that would take place in those early days and the attachments that would be formed between mother and child. If she was to continue working on Tracey's behalf, she was adamant that this bond would continue one day, when Tracey was released.

Mary had studied Tracey's case from the beginning and although she had made it clear she did not condone the level of violence involved, she had come to know Tracey and realised that, had her life taken a different turn, she could have been a good mother, a good wife and certainly a good member of society. Mary cast her mind to historic events. To Ruth Ellis, the last woman to hang in Britain in the 1950's It was a similar crime to Tracey's, a crime of passion, and horror struck her that had this taken place fifty years earlier, Tracey would have hanged!

This made Mary all the more determined to help her and to bring to people's attention the ultimate effects of domestic abuse, and the ripples it creates throughout an entire family.

Maria had just been on the 'phone again.

"O.k." she announced to Robert, as he peered over the top of his newspaper, then equally over the rim of his spectacles. "That's the buffet for the party sorted. The Moon and Stars are doing a nice selection of canapés, followed by open sandwiches – on white and granary, and some other little nibbles. I just need to confirm the choice of sweet!" Maria sifted through papers and receipts, trying to create some sort of order. Checking what was done and what needed to be done.

"I just need to confirm the booking for the limo and the timing etc., and that'll be another thing sorted. Next job is to sort the insurance on the car. Robert, could you do that for me dear? Only I have a million things to do."

"Consider it done darling," Robert sighed and returned to his newspaper.

Libby walked into the room, at first unnoticed and Maria quickly shuffled the paperwork into a folder and placed it in her desk drawer – and locked it!

"What car?" asked Libby?

"Oh nothing, just *my* car needs a little attention that's all "said Maria.

Once more Libby was suspicious, and nervous as to what it was all about. Not for one moment did she think that this subversive behaviour was anything to do with the secret plans for her party. The 'phone rang again.

"Hi Libby, It's me, Todd, you o.k. today?"

"Oh hi Todd, I'm fine. A bit bored, there's nothing to do in the country on a Sunday. Why don't you come over on the two o'clock bus, we could go for a walk?"

"O.k. yeah I could do that, see you around three then."

Libby stood on the balcony once more, the place everyone seemed to visit when in pensive mood. She loved looking out over Bradwell, with its little stone cottages nestling among the emerald green fields. It was mid-November and as she waited for Todd, there was a nip in the air. Winter was reminding her that he was beginning to rouse from his slumbers, nipping at her cheeks. The fields beyond had a shiny film of frost cast over them, and Libby thought it looked a lot like the icing sugar that Maria sprinkled on her cakes. She stared in awe at the bird table in the rockery below. The spider had spun her web across all four sides, as if she were putting up net curtains to its windows. As the frost had clothed each steely strand of the beautiful patterns, they appeared to be adorned with diamonds as they shimmered in the low sunlight. The spider was clever. The steel-like threads of her lacy home were securely anchored to all corners, and as the gentle breeze blew through them they billowed outwards, yet didn't break. Libby wondered if *she* could anchor *her* home so securely, or, in a few short weeks would its anchor become detached and her secure base be blown away. She watched with amusement as the squirrels were hurriedly looking for a spot to bury the nuts they had stolen from the bird table, completely unaware that the magpies, those policemen of the air in their blue and white feathered uniforms were watching, undercover, their vigilant surveillance about to pay off when they retrieved the booty, as the squirrel made his escape, in the misplaced belief that the nuts would still be there when he returned.

Her thoughts were interrupted by Todd's happy voice behind her. She hadn't even heard his knock at the door as Maria let him in.

"Wow what a journey!" Exclaimed Todd, "It's so foggy on the moors, you could barely see one step in front of you. I really admire the bus driver, having the guts to drive on such curly roads in these conditions."

"You get used to it out here" said Libby, almost with a derogatory tone. She flung on her jacket as they left the house for a walk by the babbling brook. They stood on the bridge and gazed into the flowing waters which were in such a hurry to move on down stream. 'Quite a contrast to my feelings' thought Libby, 'I don't want to move on so quickly.

They had barely spoken as they walked. Todd realised that Libby had something on her mind, yet she was reluctant to share it with him and he didn't want to upset her with probing questions.

The air darkened, as winter reminded her of his presence once again. The mist was now descending in the valley and as Libby raised her head, she could barely see the next little stone bridge beyond, further down the stream. She was about to tell Todd that she was in foster care, and that she didn't know where the rest of her family were, anxious to see his reaction but Winter was telling her 'not to go there.'

"I think we'd better go." Said Libby, "It can get pretty bad out here, and the weather can change very quickly.

"Yeah, I think I'll catch the next bus." Said Todd.

Libby could sense unease between them at that moment. As darkness fell, and joined the fog, the 6.15 p.m. bus pulled up at the terminus by the bridge, Todd gave Libby a little peck on her cold cheek, and climbed onto the bus. Other than this, only their frosty breath had mingled in the freezing air.

As Todd placed the palms of both hands on the bus window, Libby discreetly wiped a tear from the cheek he had kissed with her mitten, and waved to him with her other mitten clad hand as the double Decker pulled away, bound for Sheffield.

Libby didn't really know why she felt so sad, but thought it was just the moods she'd been having about her birth family lately. Or was she wondering if she would ever see Todd again. She had never realised how difficult it could be, becoming an adult.

CHAPTER ELEVEN

Maria stood by her window, sipping her morning coffee. It was much too cold to stand on the balcony today, yet as she gazed through the glass pane she could barely see the fields beyond.

"What a beautiful picture" she said.

"What's that dear?" Replied Robert as he picked up his keys in a hurry for work.

"I was just marvelling at the way in which nature paints her art. If the white window frame could now, at this very moment, be picked up and placed on the wall, what a wonderful piece of art it would be."

"If you say so dear" Robert smiled fondly, and gave his wife a goodbye hug as he left for the day ahead. Maria continued to gaze, sipping slowly at her steaming mug of coffee. She was amused by the distant landscape, changing with every minute that went by. The fog was now thick and heavy to say the least and the horizon of emerald green fields had now become a blur of charcoal coloured shapes silhouetted against the pale grey canvas of the sky, and the valley below, a basin of fluffy white mist. The little cottages were invisible. It was a work of art in monochrome. Maria thought of the story of Brigadoon, the village that disappeared in the mist. At that moment she could well have been completely alone.

Bradwell did not exist! Her mind thudded back to reality with this horrid thought of her heritage being non-existent and she was thankful for the unpredictability of the weather in the country, as the landscape changed within minutes, the fog became lighter and the faint smudged outlines of the little houses became visible, her past life was returning to her. In that moment, Maria also understood how young people like Libby and Polly *and* their siblings must feel. Their past lives were disappearing in the mists of time. But should it, as horrid as it may have been, should they be denied the jigsaw pieces, which would enable them to fit the correct shaped bits into the matching slots which would complete the whole picture of their lives?

This depressing thought prompted Maria to continue with her quest, her big surprise for Libby on her birthday, she was now feeling more determined than ever to make it happen. She loved Libby like one of her own and desperately wanted to make her happy. If only Libby knew that, and could truly believe it.

It was the day of the final L.A.C. review, and Libby was apprehensive. She had visualised this day in her head so many many times. The word 'ADULT' had floated on the air, gilded with gold and glinting in the bright lights of her mind's eye. It represented so much! It meant freedom, not only in life, but freedom from the bonds of social workers and reviews and all those embarrassing rules and regulations which had kept her shackled for most of her life. It meant she would no longer be the 'Looked after Child'. She would be grown-up! All these things she had wanted for so long, yet now, the gilded 'word' was tarnishing rapidly before her mind's eye. She was no longer so certain that this prize was what she really wanted. What would the future hold for her? Where would she end up, and how could she glue together the fragments of her past. The only person she had who truly belonged to her was Polly. How strange she thought life was. It had usually been the case that Polly was slightly envious of *her* yet at this moment the tables were turned and Libby now envied the extra year that Polly had ahead of her, still in care, protected, considered and with everyone doing their duty around her. She thought if she could just hang on for another year, she and Polly could share a flat together, but the thought was fleeting. She knew she would not be able to cope with Polly's messy ways and carefree attitude, and Polly equally would not cope with Libby's fussing and nagging her to put things away. The future was very uncertain indeed.

Libby's pensive mood was interrupted by the ringing of the doorbell and the idle chatter about the beautiful view from the window as people began to arrive. It made Libby angry that their lives were so petty that they could admire a 'view' while *her* life now hung in the balance.

Once everyone was present, the idle chatter ceased. Everyone sat silently sipping at their tea, which Maria had of course, presented in her best china cups. Grace

Marsden sat on the edge of her chair with her cup in one hand, the saucer in the other, poised dexterously beneath the cup to ensure there were no spillages on Maria's pure wool carpet. Maria sat in Robert's big winged armchair, looking slightly nervous. Libby wrongly assumed that she was worried how it would be explained that Libby must leave; make her own way, when in reality Maria's only concern was that anyone in the room could inadvertently spoil her surprise at any given moment. Mr Bramley, tutor from college sat on the sofa, looking decidedly uncomfortable perhaps because he was the only male there, and Karen the reviewing officer sat shuffling paperwork, glancing occasionally at Libby with a smile.

"O.k." said Karen, "Let's make a start shall we? Apologies first of all from Robert who can't be here due to work commitments. I'm sure he can rely on Maria to voice his opinions." She said, with a smile and a glance at Maria. "Let's begin then with education. Mr. Bramley would you care to enlighten us"

Mr Bramley proceeded to extol Libby's virtues in all areas of her education. He couldn't fault her work or presentation, and commended her commitment and dedication to the course. Then came the bit Libby hated, that of 'health!'

"So how's your health?" asked Karen.

"I'm fine. No problems" announced Libby in the vain hope that they could move on. But no, Karen had to do her bit, and ask Libby about her knowledge of contraception, where she could obtain condoms etc. clinics she could attend, and did she have any problems in that area?

Why oh why does she have to go through that every time? Libby felt her cheeks flush as she glanced at Mr Bramley, now squirming at his end of the sofa. Surely it was totally unnecessary to discuss this openly. It's private for goodness sake! Libby couldn't really decide which would be the most embarrassing actually. To divulge whether or not she was sexually active, or admit that she wasn't. It's a no-win situation she thought to herself. Then the light bulb pinged in her head, and she sat up very straight in her chair, took a deep breath and looked directly at Karen. Something came over her in that moment.

"Due to the fact that I am shortly to become an adult, I wish to make a formal complaint against social services. I feel it is entirely inappropriate that such personal and intimate matters should be discussed openly with everyone present. There should be some protocol in place whereby young people can discuss this privately and information divulged *only* to those who *need* to know. Do you people not realise how embarrassing this is for us, how demeaning?"

As the last word hung on Libby's lips, she glanced around the room. She had often heard the term 'gob-smacked' and at this precise moment, for the first time she fully understood its true meaning. Everyone in the room sat silently open-mouthed, just as though they had received a

sharp slap in the face. No-one had expected the lovely, airy-fairy, happy-go-lucky Libby, to explode in this way. Karen was the first to speak.
"Hm hm, well said, Libby. Please accept my apologies" she said, obviously now, feeling much more uncomfortable than Libby *ever* had!

"Actually Libby, I think you should make a complaint. I agree with you entirely, but we have to ask these things. Also may I suggest you consider becoming a mentor for young people in your situation? You put your case forward very eloquently indeed. Children in care need people like you to speak up for them." With that, she moved swiftly on to the next subject to be discussed that of family contact.
"What contacts do you have with your birth family Libby?"
"I have none, other than with my sister Polly." She whispered.
"And how do you feel about that dear?" sympathised Karen. At this point Maria interjected. Firstly in order to spare poor Libby's feelings, she felt she had suffered and been humiliated enough, and secondly she knew there was information she hadn't shared yet with Libby regarding her parents and really didn't want it to be blurted out now, here. Nor did she want her birthday spoiled.
"We have decided to investigate the possibility of contact after Libby's eighteenth birthday." Stated Maria, casting a knowing glance at Karen, which said 'stop right there!'

Thankfully, Karen understood and decided to bring the meeting to a close.

"However, moving on, I think it's fair to say that you will be staying with Maria and Robert for the foreseeable future, while ever you remain in education. Is that agreeable Libby?"

Libby sat back in her seat exhausted. She had never spoken out so adamantly before.

Perhaps the urgency of her situation had spurred her on to voice her opinions.

"Gosh, I really am growing up" she thought, and answered Karen with a firm "Certainly!"

With that Karen quickly shuffled her papers once more into a neat stack as she tapped them gently on her lap, and pushed her pen behind her ear. Everyone picked up their belongings and mumbled their goodbyes as Maria calmly and smilingly ushered them towards the door and waved as one by one they left the driveway. Maria closed the heavy oak front door and gave a sigh of relief as she leaned against its forgiving polished carved surface. She then took in a fresh lung full of air and returned to the living room and Libby.

"Well done darling" stated Maria. "What a stance you took, and I entirely agree. You'll go far my love." She said and ruffled Libby's hair affectionately. "Now then, get on that 'phone and arrange to meet your sister, you still need shoes and a bag to complete your birthday outfit. Go on!"

Libby was still wondering about her future. Despite what they had all said, she was confused. She put her thoughts aside and picked up the 'phone wearily.

CHAPTER TWELVE

Polly sat at the dining table staring out of the window at the white plastic garden furniture. It was now a shade of grey and the table had a little grey puddle at one side due to the legs being wobbly. John had tipped the chairs forwards, perhaps in order to avoid puddles. But no-one wanted to sit on them anymore. The yard was sludgy and the little 'postage stamp' lawn desperately needed cutting.

Polly was wondering what the outcome of Libby's review had been. She reflected on how drastically their lives had changed when they were taken into care, and here they were now, their lives about to drastically change yet again. What would become of them? She daydreamed of her brothers and sister. What did they look like now, and what were they doing, what kind of lives did they have? She could barely wait for the 'phone to ring to hear of Libby's fate. Although Polly had always envied Libby's lifestyle, deep down she wanted her to stay where she was.

Sally entered the room, and spookily read Polly's thoughts. "Don't *you* go worrying my love. They won't be taking you *anywhere* whatever happens. You're staying right here, where you belong." Stated Sally emphatically.

"Hm," thought Polly. "That's what's really important. A sense of 'belonging' something she'd never had, before meeting Sally and John.

The ringing of the 'phone, broke the silence and Polly grabbed the receiver without a blink. "Hello"
"Hi Poll," was Libby's usual response. "Thank goodness that's over! The last one, *and*, I have some advice to give you when yours comes around. Don't let them bamboozle you. Anyway, it looks like I'm staying here, for the foreseeable future anyway.
"Of course you are!" snapped Polly. "You know Robert and Maria love you to bits, they would never let you go, no matter what!"
"Well, I wasn't so sure up to a few minutes ago, but hey – I *need* shoes to go with my dress for the party, would you meet me Poll?"
An apt distraction was called for. "Yeah, if I must," droned Polly. The very thought of trudging round the shoe shops in town filled her with dread. All those strappy little sandals and needle thin heels, and silly handbags. Who needs a handbag when you have pockets? Polly felt much more confidant in a pair of the latest trainers, her combats and a bomber -jacket. She had, occasionally, wandered about her sexuality. Could she be gay? She hadn't even fancied Todd when she met him. But then again, she thought, that's perhaps as well, seeing as he was Libby's boyfriend. Yet she remembered how she'd *really* fancied her friend's brother Joe. "Oh, I don't know," she thought, time will tell, it was all very confusing.

The two girls agreed to meet on Friday, no college on Fridays which pleased Libby enormously. All day shopping for shoes, she smiled to herself. It also pleased her that it meant she would spend the day with her sister.

Friday arrived, and Libby boarded the 10.30 bus to Sheffield. A fine snow was falling up on the moors. It was *so* beautiful the way nature sifted it as it left an icing-sugar effect on the landscape. The rocks peeked through, black and sharp, the sheep struggled to walk, their woolly jackets were so thick against the elements, and little balls of snow gathered around their legs, making them look like posh poodles.
"Oh, I hope we have a white Christmas!" thought Libby. The bus pulled into the terminus and sure enough, there was Polly, waiting for her. Reliable as ever, despite being younger, Libby admitted only to herself, that Polly certainly was the more sensible one.

It was a good day together. They laughed and joked and tried their best to put their worries behind them as Libby teetered around every shoe shop in heels she could barely manage. She eventually settled for a pair of black satin sandals with a bit of bling across the front and a moderate heel which Libby could walk comfortably in. They happily found a black satin clutch bag with a pleated bow diagonally across the front which matched the shoes perfectly. Polly, surprisingly, suggested a 'bling' brooch could be placed in the centre of the bow, which would hence match the shoes even more perfectly. Libby praised Polly jokingly for her sense of girly style. All the while Polly protesting it was just a hunch. Therefore, in happy mood the girls hugged each other goodbye, as Libby boarded the bus to return to the Styx.

Back at home Maria had taken advantage of Libby's absence in order to perfect a few of her plans for the 'Party of the Year'. She had made umpteen 'phone calls, had endless notes in front of her and her arm was aching from holding the 'phone to her ear for so long. But she sat back in her chair, put the top on her pen and daydreamed as she stretched her aching arms above her head and brought them to rest clasped together at the back of her neck. She gazed out of the window and tried to visualize each step of the party arrangements. The table décor, the flowers, the menu, the guest list etc., etc., and was happy that the day had been fruitful. She reflected upon the experience she'd had, doing similar events for her own daughters, and she loved Libby no less.

As she sat there, musing as to how successfully or not, the party would go, in walked Libby.
"I'm home!"
"How did it go?" asked Maria, but she could see from Libby's face, *and* the numerous carrier bags weighing down her shoulders, that the trip had been successful.
"Now, I have everything to wear for the party." Smiled Libby, as she flopped into the chair and kicked off her shoes relieving her aching feet.
"Oh, I'm so excited Maria. It's going to be wonderful, I can't wait."

"Not long now darling" said Maria, bathing contentedly in her foster daughter's happy glow. Bathing, yes. "Why don't you go and have a nice hot bath and an early night dear, you look exhausted."

"But so do you Maria. What *have* you been doing lately? You look worn out. *I* know! Why don't *you* have a bath and an early night? You deserve it for putting up with me lately! C'mon, I'll go and run it for you."

"Perhaps I will." Answered Maria with a weary smile. Her work was done! Perhaps now she felt she could relax, or could she? Her mind was still racing with thoughts and plans. As she sank back into the warm scented water, she pushed the button of the Jacuzzi bath and wallowed in lavender bubbles.

First of December, 8. a.m. There was no sun to wake Libby today and as she stirred and stretched, only a grey gloom slid through the chink in the curtains. Yet as she pulled back the duvet and shuffled over to the window, there was an odd brightness, and as she pulled back the stubborn curtains, the odd brightness fully revealed itself. It had snowed!

"Oh, how lovely, perhaps we'll have a white Christmas." She thought happily. As she marvelled at the fresh bright cleanness of the landscape before her, Libby suddenly realised that there would be a lot to do today and Maria would certainly be in need of her help. She dashed down the stairs and into the kitchen.

"Morning Maria!" She chuckled. "What would you like me to do?"

"Well, you can get this down you for a start dear, you need a good breakfast inside you with all the work we have today."

"Gosh, I feel more like a bride on her wedding day" Libby giggled. Then her smile fell, as thoughts of Todd crossed her mind. She missed him, hadn't seen him for a couple of weeks. She *genuinely* missed him, and wondered why Bridal chat had brought him to mind, because strangely, where Todd was concerned, marriage would never be on the cards. No, she felt she cared for him in a different way. As a best buddy perhaps. She was, however still quite miffed that he felt someone else was more important than she today. It must be someone very special she thought, and a slight tinge of envy touched her. This was unusual for Libby. She normally didn't have a jealous bone in her body. She'd never had the need, she had always been happy with her lot in life. Perhaps deep down she felt that everything she now had, was far better than anything she'd had previously with Tracey and Darren. With that, her thoughts immediately were focussed upon her birth parents, and siblings.

"I wonder where Tracey and Darren are now." She asked Maria sadly.

Maria was stunned by Libby's sudden poignant question and felt a slight pang of panic. "Oh, no – not today of all days." She knew both Libby and Polly had always referred to their birth parents by their first names, rather than Mum or Dad. It was almost as though these honourable titles had to be earned, and they had not been. They had a unique definition which she felt did not apply to Tracey and Darren. "I expect *after* today you can go and find out everything you need to know. Though, it may not altogether be very nice you know I just want you to be prepared dear." Maria knew she was just trying to take these thoughts away from Libby, just for today, yet at the same time she knew she had a duty to her foster daughter, and felt it was appropriate to prepare her for the awful facts she would discover, very shortly.

"Right!" Said Maria sharply, lifting the grim mood which had been gradually descending.

"You, my girl, can tuck into that" as she placed a huge cooked breakfast on the table in front of Libby, followed by a large mug of tea. Come on now get it down you. Then, when you've finished that, all *you* have to do today, is make yourself even more beautiful than usual, if that's possible."

Libby gave a strained little smile and silently thanked the Lord for such a wonderful person as Maria.

"I think I'll just go and give Polly a ring, see what she's wearing tonight, she never told me" she announced indignantly.

"Hi, Poll, what you up to?" She muttered as runny egg made its way slowly down her chin.

"Hi Lib, I'm just ironing my jeans for tonight!" Polly replied, with a taunting tone in her voice. Libby bit!

"Polly McIntyre, if you turn up at my party wearing jeans, I'll strangle you!"

"Only kidding."

"What *are* you wearing?" queried Libby.

"Now, that would be telling, you'll have to wait and see, I'm sure I can dig something from the bottom of my wardrobe." Laughed Polly, happy that she had just shocked Libby out of her obviously grim mood.
"Come on Lib. It's your big day today, cheer up."
"I'm sorry Poll, I was just thinking about Tracey and Darren this morning."
"Well don't! I never think about them." Scolded Polly. Now go and have a nice soak in that ridiculous 'bubbly' thingy in your bathroom. I'll see you later."
Libby mentally agreed, replaced the receiver and slowly climbed the stairs, her mind racing. 'Let me see, hairdresser at two, nails at three thirty, plenty of time.'

CHAPTER THIRTEEN

Maria arrived at the Moon and Stars at 7.p.m. She wanted to check that preparations were going smoothly. Robert had remained at home to watch over Libby and to escort her to the venue for the evening. He also felt it was a great excuse to keep out of the proceedings as much as possible. As she entered the function room, the layout looked amazing. The gilt chairs with their red velvet seats were perfect she thought. The tables were laid immaculately and the red napkins drew it all together. She approached the kitchen doorway and asked if she could view the food on the menu. Maria was suitably impressed. There was a banquet before her eyes. It was a veritable cornucopia of the most scrumptious food. The champagne, the best, would be like nectar to the Gods. She smiled and nodded; totally satisfied that everything was in order. Her only hope was that the rest of her plans, the nerve-racking conclusion to weeks of stress and hard work, would also be as perfect.

Maria looked at her watch. "Gosh, the guests will be arriving soon!" She made her way to the centre of the room for one last look at the setting, clasped her hands and smiled with satisfaction once more, then made her way to the doorway to greet the guests as they arrived. There were many, Libby was an extremely popular girl. Eventually, Sally and John arrived with Billy and Bruce, all spruced up with their hair combed and parted. Sally looked wonderful, though motherly as she was, and John wore his usual brown suit, kept for special occasions. Polly looked amazing! Maria could not believe her eyes. She wore a little black mini dress which showed off a pair of beautiful legs which had clearly not been shown to the outside world before, as Polly kept nervously tugging at the hem of her 'nearly' dress. Her blond short curly hair was tucked behind her ears, a little glittery band holding it in place, and there was even a glimmer of lip gloss. Maria was so very pleased that Polly had made such an effort. Not only for Libby, but little did she realise at this point, that this evening would be almost as important for her too.

Back at the house, Libby was putting the finishing touches to her makeup and smoothing her long hair into place, when Robert called to her "Taxi's here!"
Libby grabbed her little black clutch bag from the dressing table, took a deep breath as she scanned one last glance at her reflection in the mirror and slowly descended the steps to her waiting taxi.
"You look stunning!" Said Robert with pride as he took her hand and gently kissed her on the cheek. As she reached the last step, after carefully watching every single one, so as not to trip, her eyes widened. There in front of her was a huge, stretch, *PINK* limo! She felt like 'Princess Libby' on her way to the ball, though she knew there would be no Prince Charming yet despite this she was deliriously happy. She knew nothing of Maria's waiting surprise.

The limo travelled slowly, Libby hanging her head out of the window, waving to everyone passing by.
"Gosh, how 'chav', she thought, just as they arrived at the Moon and Stars. The driver, in full livery, stepped out and opened the door for 'Princess Libby.' She gently lifted her dress slightly and placed her sandaled foot onto the pavement, as the driver took her hand in his and tipped his cap with the other.

Everyone gasped as they watched from the windows. Not only at the Pink Limo, but at the sight of Libby. She was a vision, a dream to behold. She was wearing a dress of the most vivid red flowing organza, the strapless bodice which was of the blackest, deepest velvet, clung to her perfect frame. A little tiara glinted, as it nestled amongst the shiny strands of her hair. Everyone was aghast!
"Oh, Lib', you look *GORGEOUS!*" Announced Polly. "No wonder you didn't tell anyone what you were wearing, they're all gob-smacked."
"Well look at you." Replied Libby, "Where did those legs come from? You dark horse."

Everyone was led to their seats, as soft music played in the background. Libby took her place at the centre table. As hushed conversation spread around the room, Maria approached the microphone, placed at the front of the stage. As the soft music ceased, and silence descended upon the room, Maria began to speak nervously.
"First of all, thank you so much to everyone for coming this evening; it's a very special one. Not only for Libby, but

also for Robert, Fiona and Harriet and myself. Libby has brought a sparkle to all of our lives and we feel very blessed to have cared for her for these past few years." Libby began to blush, her soft cheeks, now almost the colour of her dress, but Maria continued. "Most of you here, who know Libby, will also be aware that, she and Polly haven't seen any of their birth family for many years." Maria could now see that Libby was beginning to feel decidedly uncomfortable, which was definitely *not* Maria's intention. She decided the best thing would be to cut short her carefully prepared speech forthwith and beckoned Libby *and* Polly up onto the stage. This hadn't gone according to plan at all, and with the hand of each girl in hers, Maria just blurted it out.

"I have been doing a great deal of detective work, along with Grace Marsden and Anna Faraday, who are also here tonight. Please, will you join us?" Whereupon Grace, and Anna joined them on the stage. Polly and Libby, both, were perplexed, and stood together in awe, all the while Polly was tugging at the hem of her dress, unnecessarily ashamed of the beautiful legs no-one had ever seen. Maria continued.

"I know that both of you girls have often wondered about your birth family, for a while now and we felt it was time to do something about that and although we can't bring *all* of them to you, we can bring *some* of them a little closer." As Maria said the last word, a woman unknown to Polly and Libby ushered a young girl towards them. She was about twelve years old and looked a little familiar.

"This is your sister, Beth!" Said Maria with a voice that faltered and was in great danger of bursting into a sob. Libby was awestruck, and with both hands covering the lower half of her face, in order to stifle and conceal her emotions, she took slow certain steps towards her new-found sibling, followed by Polly who was trying as always to hold it together. The three of them now stood, locked in a group hug which spanned the missing years.

Maria was already beginning to wonder if she had done the right thing, when in walked a young man, dressed in a suit, having made a great effort to meet his sisters after so long.
"This is your brother, Jared."
The siblings were overcome with joy, though very tearful, but this made Maria feel that all would eventually be o.k. She hoped so with all her heart.
"As you will each now be aware, this leaves only your eldest brother Todd. Todd is all grown up now and proved a little more difficult to find. However, find him we did!" Clapped Maria, as a very handsome Todd approached them.
Libby and Polly turned as they wiped their very tear-filled eyes, their jaws dropping in disbelief. Yes, Todd *was* indeed handsome, despite the little scars on his cheek, the same scars SCOTT had on *his* face from the broken glass which splintered, caused when he had broken the tumbler that day, many moons ago. But what struck the girls the most was his uncanny likeness to Scott! In fact, it *was* Scott!! Naturally, he too was speechless. At birth each

child had been given two names. One chosen by Darren and one chosen by Tracey. Scott's second name was Todd, and following his adoption, he had made a bold decision. In an effort to forget the past, for being the eldest he remembered more than the others, he had elected to call himself by his second name, Todd.

Maria, for once, was also speechless when she set eyes on Scott. She had carried out all communication verbally with Social Services and a mediator and had never actually set eyes on any of these siblings, until tonight. What an irony.

Libby was *so* happy. Not only was she having the party of her life, but her brothers and sisters were all here with her tonight. But what made her the happiest of all was the fact that Todd, or Scott, had given up everything to be with them tonight. Even, as he had thought, the Libby he was growing to love, in order to be with the sister he longed to see. Now, he had both in one package. It had broken his heart too that he couldn't be with her yet here he now was, *with* Libby, not previously knowing she was his sister. This explained the feelings and the attraction he and Libby had for one another. Why they couldn't fathom it. Who would have? Polly too was so happy. She'd had feelings for Todd that she couldn't explain also and now she knew what those feelings were, she could at last slot them into place. They were those invisible invincible emotions between brothers and sisters, which could not be denied even through time and space.

Following this there was *nothing* more Maria could do that would shock or amaze Libby on this very special occasion.

Or was there? The two girls were so emotionally swept off their feet, they hadn't picked up on the clue that Maria had given them when she'd announced that not *all* of their siblings were there. They knew nothing as yet of baby Max. But she felt there was enough to cope with for one night. Besides, given Max's circumstances and his young age that was as yet beyond even Maria's powers of persuasion.

Maria took the microphone in her hand once more and a hush fell over the entire room.
"There is just one thing I forgot in all of this excitement. That of your birthday present!" With that Maria offered Libby a small box, wrapped in glittering paper, with a little curly bow on the top. Maria had a knack when it came to making things look beautiful. Libby took the box, said a quiet thank you and kissed Maria and Robert. She was pleased that they had bought her perhaps a pendant, or a ring to mark the occasion, but the *best* present ever had been having her family returned to her. As Libby began carefully to un-wrap the tiny gift, she was being gently ushered towards the door. She found this slightly irritating as she struggled with the ribbon and the sticky tape. Once she had won her battle with the wrappings, she was slightly perplexed to see a key, hiding in the cotton wool, lining the box, but as she looked up questioningly, her queries were answered. There before her, on the road outside, stood a shiny red car! The key fitted perfectly.
"Oh!" Shrieked Libby. "I know I felt like Cinderella tonight, but instead of a shoe fitting, it's a key!" She clapped her

hands in glee. "Now I can get to Uni' a whole lot quicker every day,"
"You need to pass your driving test first dear." Came Robert's practical reply.

The whole evening went with a resounding bang! Everyone enjoyed themselves, and as for these young people who had found each other again, well, there were no words to describe their emotions. As the music faded, the balloons withered and the sumptuous food was reduced to crumbs, it was time to go home. As Libby stepped outside as they left the Moon and Stars, she felt decidedly chilly. Winter! He was nipping her, reminding her of his presence. As she looked skywards, little soft snowflakes were tickling the tip of her nose as they fell to earth, like loose feathers from Angel's wings falling earthbound and discarded. She shivered as he ran an Icicle finger up her spine. Her strapless dress was no match for his cloak of ice, yet she had all the love that was tumbling from this place to keep her warm tonight. She and Todd and Jared and Polly had all agreed to meet up again, and Beth too if her adoptive parents would allow. They needed to get to know each other and fill in some pieces of the puzzle which had been their lives so far.

Maria knew the questions would now come thick and fast, like knives being flung in the air. But she also knew she had to answer them and it wasn't going to be pleasant. She suddenly felt a pang of pain in her heart on behalf of Tracey. *She* should have been here tonight. How must she feel, locked away in her grey room, knowing all of her children were growing into adults, and she was missing it all?

Maria decided to ask for permission to write to Tracey. To tell her about Libby's party, how she had grown from a beautiful child into a stunning young woman and how well she was doing at Uni. Maria didn't know Tracey at all, but felt that, if in no other way than guardianship and love of Libby, they shared a tenuous bond.

CHAPTER FOURTEEN

Tracey was feeling extremely nervous and bewildered. She was being moved to a mother and baby unit within the prison. Max was thriving – and growing. There were mixed feelings for Tracey. On the one hand she was grateful that the baby *was* thriving and that so far, she had been allowed to keep him, yet she knew it was only a matter of time before they would cruelly take him away from her. She understood, of course. Who would want a child to grow up within this austere place? No, she knew he would be taken. Just as her other babies had been taken. Once again she could not take in the irony of it all. She reminisced as to how difficult, almost impossible it had been to bond, and care for her children, under the overbearing influence and selfishness of Darren. Yet here in her captivity she was caring for Max extremely well, *and* loving him more with each day that passed, and yet still they would steal him from her. She was also well aware that it was Libby's birthday today; she had written her a letter, telling her how she loved her and how much she missed her. She had made a little card, drawn hearts all over it and put eighteen little kisses beneath Libby's name. Little did she know that Maria had held it back until tomorrow.

Tracey sobbed, as she tried to visualize each one of her children, and speculated as to how they would look now, grown up, adults, some of them. It saddened her, reminiscing about what she had missed. Little Max gave a cry and immediately Tracey snapped out of her thoughts and responded to his needs. She was going to be a *good* mother this time, to little Max. No-one was going to take him away from her – permanently. She would do whatever she had to do. However, she trembled at the thought of how out of control she was, stuck in here. What if they put him in foster care and the people decided to keep him? Tracey had no knowledge of how the system worked, and it worried her. She realised how different things would be for her and this baby. There was no Darren for a start, though she felt great remorse at having taken his life. Also, there were people to show her how to care for her baby properly and support her, and she would always put him first. She loved him so much which actually made his imminent departure all the more earth shattering. The heartache would be doubly painful come their parting. What about the people who would take him? They wouldn't understand how she felt. How, could they measure her pain? They were just doing their jobs and all these people who also cared for her other children. Were they caring for her children properly? Though how dare she even think otherwise. They didn't know her, what a wicked, evil woman she was who didn't care about or love her children. A murderer!

So many thoughts were jangling in her head, and in her prison cell there was little to do to create a distraction, and so they grew out of all proportion. Her fears grew with every passing day. Each time she heard a prison door slam, she'd physically jump, and her heart would race, assuming they were coming to take Max from her. A man or woman in the condemned cell could not have suffered more fear than Tracey felt with each passing day. She held Max tightly, cuddling him, singing to him. When would they come?

Her cell door opened, and she trembled, clinging to Max with all her strength, and fear in her eyes.

"It's o.k. Tracey!' Soothed the prison guard. "I've told you, they will make arrangements for Max and let you know when he will be going. He'll be fine, he'll be well taken care of until you're released."

Tracey couldn't be sure, her other children were taken into care and they never came back. She felt so helpless, and so very insecure. Another irony, she thought. How much *more* secure could one feel behind prison bars.

There was a loud rap on her cell door and in walked another prison guard. One not so kind, who took great delight in demoralising her charges at any given opportunity.

"There's mail for you McIntyre." She snapped in her derogatory tone.

Tracey snapped out of her internal world and looked up anxiously as the warder handed her a crumpled buff envelope, slit open at the top. This was yet another violation, degradation, as everything had to be checked and read for its content before being handed over to an inmate. However Tracey knew this was a necessary procedure, another part of the consequences of losing her liberty. It somehow sullied the treasure within, made it feel second-hand. Nonetheless, Tracey took it eagerly. She peered into the darkness of the envelope, pulling apart the slit open top. It was hardly the same as feeling the excitement of ripping open the envelope herself, rather like the excitement of pulling a Christmas cracker and the anticipation of what might be within. There was however *some* excitement attached to it. Or was it fear? Who could be writing to her she wondered? Could it be another 'do-gooder' on the outside, wishing to impart Christian love? She peered once more into the envelope before removing any of its contents, almost as though something might give her a clue, but try as she may, it was necessary to pull the bundle within from the safety of its buff cocoon out into the sultry air. As she slowly grasped the contents a batch of photographs fell to the floor like a deck of cards. They hadn't even replaced them safely. She picked them up hastily, not wanting them to be contaminated even further by their contact with the cell floor, but first she opened the folds of the good quality writing paper which had once safely wrapped them like caring loving arms. The letter was hand-written, that was encouraging. There were several pages too; somebody must be interested in her! This was a new and warming experience for Tracey. She decided to read the letter before she looked at any of the photos. That way she would know better who or what they were. The writing was clear and in a beautiful hand.

'Hello Tracy, my name is Maria, and along with my husband Robert, I am Foster Carer to your daughter Libby..............

Tracey read it, and then read it again. It was a beautiful letter with encouraging words, all about her daughter Libby.

When Tracey had digested every word, twice, she picked up the photos. Horror, washed over her like a tidal wave! All she could see was a girl, resembling herself, in a *red* organza dress. The memories of that fateful night, the red dress she herself had worn, the blood, oh the copious blood – RED!! She dropped the pictures on the floor as though they themselves were the weapon she had used to rip Darren's flesh and backed herself up to the cold grey wall, sobbing. She was in turmoil, and at first her thoughts were bitter towards Maria. Who *did* this woman think she was? She'd had *my* daughter all these years. She had seen her grow, rather than me! Tracey sat back down with a thud. What a strange feeling to be hearing from someone who had cared for her child all these years.

Someone who was doing the job, *she* herself should have done. She didn't know how to feel, jealous or grateful. How *should* she feel, she didn't know. She continued to read Maria's letter, explaining about Libby's birthday, how lovely it was and how Libby had wished Tracey could have been there. Maria also described the reunion with Todd, Jared and Beth, and how Libby and Polly see each other regularly. It was a lengthy letter and Tracey had to go back to the beginning and read it all over again in order to take it all in. She then picked up the photographs sitting sadly on her grey prison blanket and began to sift through them. Maria had written carefully on the back of each one, explaining who everyone was. Tracey didn't know any of these young men and women before her eyes, they were adults, not her babies, the children she left behind. She traced the outlines of their faces with her finger as she searched for the child in each of them. Her tears fell like rain and wrinkled the picture she held. Eventually she again reached the birthday picture of Libby in all her glory. The one Robert had taken in the hallway that night before he escorted her to the party. Tracey screamed yet again, with a blood curdling echo, the warder came running and the shouting and laughing of the inmates ceased abruptly.

"The red, the red, the dress!" Shouted Tracey as she glared at Libby's red organza gown, reminiscent of the red she had worn the night her beloved Max and the hated Darren had died. It was also the last ever garment she had worn prior to her prison grey. She cried for hours, and Max cried with her, sensing his mother's distress. When

120

her body ached so much, she could cry no more, she picked up the pictures and looked slowly through them once again. This time she actually saw the beautiful girl that was her daughter, of all her children and her first born, Scott. She was heartbroken yet at the same time deliriously happy to see these images of them, to know that they had all been together in one place. Together!" This was the key word which swam round and round in Tracey's head; all she had were her thoughts. She made a grand decision there and then. She was going to work towards getting out of prison, she would appeal. This correspondence had given her new hope. Although she and Maria had never met, the two women had a bond from afar. Tracey no longer felt Maria was a threat; she had *cared* for her daughter all these years. Perhaps she could reply. Perhaps Maria would visit her, or perhaps not. *This* was what prison was all about. Losing your liberty, your freedom to do what you want or go where you wanted, to have choices. Tracey sat at her table and began a heartrending reply to Maria. She could now see the value of foster care. These people were *not* taking her children, they were borrowing them, bridging the gap in whatever the circumstances, and they were an asset to people like her. What would have happened otherwise?

CHAPTER FIFTEEN

Maria and Robert were feeling the strain now that the party was over. All those months of planning and executing the surprises had taken its toll. The children had now been given the news about Tracey and Darren. Those old enough asked to see their files at Social Services, to enable them to take it all in and make sense of it. Libby had also bombarded Maria with questions. Sally and John were feeling much the same. They too, still had the responsibility of Polly.

Maria decided in her usual positive manner, that they needed a break. Libby was able to look after herself for a week. The neighbours in the village would keep a watchful eye on her too. Robert and Maria had a villa on the island of Tenerife and invited John and Sally to join them for a holiday. Libby was now eighteen and it was decided that Polly could stay with her; it would give the pair of them a little responsibility. To see what life would be like on their own, yet under the ever watchful gaze of neighbour Mrs. Jones. Billy and Bruce had gone to stay with an aunt, giving Sally and John the much needed break they also deserved. Although it was perilously close to Christmas, Maria felt she had everything under control, as usual.

It was a bitterly cold December morning when they boarded the 'plane in their winter woollies. They were all in happy mood and ready for some sun. As the 'plane reached take-off, Maria then, and only then, began to relax. She leaned back and closed her eyes and thought back over the last few weeks, and how fraught they had been and yet with her determination, and the diligent co-operation of Grace Marsden, she had pulled off nothing short of a miracle.

"I don't know how you did it Maria." Cooed Sally

"Neither do I, if truth be known Sally, it was worth it though, don't you think?"

"Absolutely!"

Within hours they were landing on the sun drenched tarmac of paradise, exhausted but happy. The next day they sat around the blue, cool inviting pool, didn't want to overdo things too soon. Maria lay on her sun-lounger gazing at the azure blue of the sky. Little white, wispy, feathery clouds drifted by above her, like little Angels saying: - "You did great, now relax!" Maria tried, here on the 'Island of Eternal Spring' with its barren yet fascinating, lunar landscape. She tried to distract herself, examining the tops of the volcanoes, and marvelling at the way in which each one had a little puff of pure white cloud above its crater, which never seemed to move. 'Why is that?' she wondered, as if by having to examine the reason for this, she could implant another, different thought other than those which were already crowding and invading her mind and there really was no space for this irrelevant one. There were too many, the situation at home was still like a ticking time bomb, waiting to explode when the whole truth about the children's lives and family, finally hit them. Everything was so very fragile and Maria felt as though she was holding an indulgent bouquet of broken glass shards in her hands, and the tighter she gripped to hold it all together, the deeper it cut.

She fidgeted on her sun-lounger, adjusting it up, then down, needing the welcome shade of the parasol lest the cruel, yet welcome sun should fry her already overheated brain. The four of them did silly relaxing things that didn't tax the brain. They walked on the beach, they ate delicious seafood and drank intoxicating wine. They chatted endlessly about anything and everything *except* the situation at home. Everyone was deliberately avoiding it in an outward attempt to *relax*, blot it out. They even did the fun trip on the submarine in the bay. Maria felt a sudden wave of dread as the vessel began to descend beneath the waves, into a silent watery world where everything seemed to move in slow motion. There were stingray and barracuda swimming around confidently and peering at these humans through the porthole windows. The tables were turned, and Maria understood how fish must feel when we peer at *them* in a goldfish bowl. For a brief moment she felt trapped, couldn't escape, she was in their world now, and they had the freedom. She also realised how Tracey must feel in her cell, trapped in a goldfish bowl full of sharks. Quite an analogy, yet it gave her a deep sense of empathy.

As the wonderful week drew to a close, everyone's thoughts turned to the situation at home. Christmas was just around the corner. Despite the sunshine and clear blue sky here, there were constant reminders at every turn. A beautifully bedecked Christmas tree stood by the side of the grand piano in the corner of the restaurant. The welcome sun glinted on the tinsel draped between the trees on the beach front, and glistened on the tips of tiny waves on the ocean which resembled a waft of deep blue velvet scattered with diamonds. A contradiction in terms of what they would find back in England in the middle of December, yet Maria could hardly wait to get home. There was one more plan in the making; would she pull it off she thought?

The adults had been in contact with the kids back home, several times a day to check they were o.k. but Maria had been on the 'phone more than most. As she had stood on the balcony to make calls, only a muffled voice could be heard, but her body language said she was laying down the law, and Sally and John were a little concerned that anything could be so important that it should intrude on Maria's holiday.

"Just stuff to do with work, I expect" waffled Robert.

But Sally and John felt it was more than that. Sitting in the restaurant the night before their return home, all thoughts turned to Christmas.

"We've bought Polly that bright pink I Pod she's been after" smiled Sally.

"She'll be pleased with that. Any chance you all might like to join us at home for Christmas dinner?" Asked Maria inquisitively.

"Oh, that would be wonderful." Sally replied, rather relieved that the effort of cooking such an important meal had been lifted from her. Whilst Sally loved baking bread, and cakes', cooking for a large number of people was not her forte, therefore she was overjoyed and readily accepted before John could draw breath, with *his* opinion.

It had been a bumpy flight home from Tenerife, a lot of air turbulence and the weather was not good as they approached England. As they stepped out of the Terminal Building, sighs of pleasure filled the air. It was snowing! Softly snowing, there was an air of quietness all around for footsteps could not be heard as people scurried on the soft, white, carpet to their taxis. Tenerife had been beautiful and the sun had worked overtime there as he deserted his duties back in England, but here on British soil, Winter had taken over and brought a beauty of his own. He was in full competition with this soft silent shower and already scoring points, as everyone returning from the heat, smiled with joy.

Back home the girls were so excited at the return of their loving foster carers. Their week alone had been long and had been an ideal test of love. Having had to do *everything* for themselves, they now realised how loved they were, and how much they loved in return, *and* how fortunate they were to have been rescued from their previous hellish lives, and despite the bitter cold outside, Libby felt a warm glow in her heart at the thought of Robert and Maria's return. Whilst their carers had been away, Libby had decided to go and read her files, the case conferences, L.A.C. reviews, and court decisions. She soon realised she should have waited for Maria. She was eighteen, so what? Did that mean she was more grown up that day, than she was the day before? As she read the transcript of what had happened between her birth parents, and the subsequent outcome, Libby was devastated. She didn't know how to handle it all. There were mixed emotions. Blame, guilt, sympathy, loss, fear, all rolled into one big snowball, yet another fragile bouquet of glass, the sharp edges tearing at her heart. Was Darren to blame for his treatment of Tracey? Was Tracey to blame for killing Darren, leaving her with no parents at all, good or bad? So many questions were hitting her head like a pin-ball machine. Libby was so glad Maria and Robert would be home today. What was *more* difficult was trying not to discuss what she had read about, with her younger sister. Polly was not ready.

Polly approached Libby on the balcony, where she was standing, deep in thought, the soft snowflakes forming a cooling hand on her boiling brain. She gazed down at the houses in the village below. Their rooftops now softly white, resembling little cakes which Winter had deftly dusted with an icing sugar effect, peaceful, quiet.

"What you doin' out ere?" asked Polly with teeth chattering "It's freezing you'll catch yer' death!"

'Huh!' thought Libby, 'Death.'

As she looked skywards as though searching for the 'plane carrying her carers, soft white snowflakes fell once more on the tip of her nose, comforting like little angel feathers telling her she was loved, bringing mercy. Down in the village she could see the lights twinkling on the Christmas tree which the council had put up by the bridge. The finger of God was clad in his white winter coat of pure virgin snow and was barely visible silhouetted against the snow filled sky. It reminded her it was almost Christmas. Goodwill to all men, cheer and happiness and all that. She felt she really must get her head around it all, it was snapping at her heels. She turned, wrapped her fluffy dressing gown tightly around her glowing heart and shuffled her fluffy slippered feet back inside. She and Polly sat down with tea and toast awaiting the return of their guardians, their protectors, their loved ones.

CHAPTER SIXTEEN

Tracey was still the timid little mouse, everybody's victim. She often welcomed her prison cell as a refuge from the shouting and fighting that was a daily occurrence here. She just wanted to get her head down, do her time and become free to see her children.

Christmas was bitter-sweet for her. It was a family time but with a very distant fragmented family, though she did her best to get through it. Santa's red coat was yet again a reminder of the 'red.' She could not free her mind of her red dress, Max's red tie, the red triangle of blood which dominated her thoughts. There was little doubt Tracey needed therapeutic input, yet she had been given none. Apart from this the only thought which filled her mind was that Max, her baby son had now been taken from her, torn from her reaching arms. They had given her one day's notice. Twenty-four short hours to impart all the love within her heart, to her infant son, before he would be gone. Gone for how long she didn't know. Her desperate cries ignored, her heartache left to grow sharper and sharper, her arms vacant and empty.

It was Christmas Eve, and down in the village both church and chapel were preparing for midnight Mass. The tall Christmas tree by the bridge was proudly displaying its brightly coloured fairy lights, doubly effective as they were reflected in the waters of the babbling brook. As the snow fell, it left an eerie silence in the air, and again, footsteps could not be heard as they trod on the soft white carpet. The huge puddle by Brook Buildings which had always proved an obstacle to Libby as a child was now frozen solid. She trod on it in defiance of the number of times it had soaked her feet and it cracked like fragile glass into a thousand pieces. Just like her present life. She had her foster family whom she loved dearly, her newly discovered birth siblings whom presented yet another fragment of her life. Then there was her birth mother, a murderess, incarcerated for however long, with an infant whom Libby may never know, and to top all this, Libby had noticed Maria's subversive manner at times. Could she be planning for Libby to move on? After all, she was now an adult, she *should* be ready to become independent, but Libby just didn't want to be. She was beginning to realise that Maria and her family meant more to her than just foster parents alone, she actually felt great affection for them, deep down.

She shivered as the cold air brought her to her senses, as other young people could be heard chatting as they gathered together, collecting their torches, and preparing to light them to proceed on their journey from one end of the village to the other. The practice had some Pagan origin which few could even remember. It was just a tradition which was ceremoniously practiced each year without a second thought, though happily it somehow brought the whole village together in one thought and deed. Sadly these days, most were too busy taking advantage of the extended drinking time in the pub to be bothered, but Libby felt duty bound to keep to tradition. The brass band struck up to the tune of Hark the Herald Angels Sing and everyone began to move in unison. Left right, left right, in accordance with the base drum.

Back up the lane, at home, Maria was making final preparations for tomorrow. Placing the gifts under the tree, making sure they were well labelled to each and every one in the family. Fiona and Harriet were coming home for a couple of days. In the dining room, Maria had laid the table. Tomorrow, she would need the large oak dining table with its folding oak leaves fully extended. There would be herself and Robert, Harriet and Fiona, Libby, Polly and John and Sally, and Billy and Bruce. Scott and Jared had been invited. Beth naturally was staying at home with her adoptive family, but then Maria laid an extra place.

"I think you've laid one too many Maria. Easily done when there are so many." Laughed Libby.

"No no, we have a couple of extra guests for Christmas Dinner this year."

"And who might that be?"

"All will be revealed tomorrow. It's late, let's go to bed!"

Maria took one last glance at the dining room before retiring for the night. 'A job well done' she thought, as she surveyed the long oak table. It was a picture, the best china was laid, the napkins suitably 'origamied' and the silver shone brighter than the pieces of the brass band she'd just heard. It was 1.a.m. 'Huh, Christmas Day already' she thought. The birth of our Lord, a special day. Would the following hours be special or would they be a total disaster? She stood for a moment out on the balcony and decided to finish the brandy she had poured. Now feeling that maybe she needed the extra courage for the day's events. She hated being so secretive about things, but if truth be known, she never quite knew how or even if these tenuous threads would knit together, therefore she always felt it best that no-one knew what was happening until they happened, then there would be no disappointment. She gazed upwards as her misty breath disappeared into the night. She watched the icicle stars twinkling in the frozen ocean sky, where was the North Star? She felt glad she couldn't see it, after all it would have led Herod to the infant, to kill him and we would have had no saviour. Wasn't this allegedly the season of Peace and Goodwill? How much of that is there left in the world? Still, tomorrow's secret guest had love and understanding, a giving heart and her name was well deserved Maria mused. However she needed sleep, there was a busy day ahead tomorrow. Enough cynicism.

The eerie light of the snow clad hills peeked through Libby's curtains. The clock glowed in number shapes of 7 a.m. in the darkness of the room. She stirred and remembered it was Christmas Day! She got out of bed with more enthusiasm than usual, flung her fleecy dressing gown over her shoulders and crossed it tightly around her, holding it there with her arms, against the cold. Sliding her feet into her fluffy slippers, she tiptoed her way through to the kitchen. She was *slightly* surprised to see that she was not the first up and about. Maria was already busy preparing the turkey, chopping veggies and making sure everything would run smoothly. Maria was good at everything she did and Libby was therefore confidant that today's events – whatever they were, would be no exception. Libby sprinted into the living room as quickly as her fluffy slippers would allow. The tree looked resplendent in all its glory, its little fairy lights glinting in the dim morning light. All the gifts were arranged, by Maria of course, around its lower branches and Libby knelt on the floor and began reading the labels on each of them until she found those bearing her name. There were various wonderful things from the family, neighbours and friends, and then one very tiny box from Maria and Robert. Libby wasn't sure how to feel about its tinyness, but then she remembered the box she received for her birthday, containing a small key – to her car. She unwrapped the gift, slowly and carefully removing the shimmering little bow so as not to damage it. It contained a small jewel box made of black leather. Robert, who had now emerged, and Maria, sat with bated breath waiting for the treasure inside to be revealed. Libby lifted the lid, to see one of the rarest gems known to man. A.A.A.

Tanzanite! A thousand times rarer than diamonds. It was also her birthstone and the deepest purple colour. This was something Libby had coveted for so long, but never dreamt she could own, something very precious which encompassed her value to the Sinclairs. She was overjoyed.

As the morning progressed, Libby helped Maria to put the finishing touches to the table, whilst Robert cleared the deep snow from the path with his big red snow shovel. Maria asked Libby to start lighting the festive candles around the dining room. She turned the central heating up a notch, as she realised everyone would feel the bitter cold of the countryside as they arrived. She wanted to create a warm and welcoming ambience for her guests and for one in particular.

Fiona and Harriet were first to arrive, surreptitiously asking mum if there was anything they could do to help; of course hoping all the while that there really wouldn't be, as they sat down with a glass of wine.

The snow in Sheffield was not so picturesque. The traffic speeding by had created little waves by the roadside topped with mud, yet they were pretty in their own way. Polly looked out of her bedroom window at the rooftops across the street to assess the weather for their journey to The Peak District. She looked down at their little yard. Billy and Bruce had built a snowman. She was angry with them for their juvenile cheekiness, as Sally had given them a carrot for a nose, but they had chosen to put it elsewhere as they stood giggling, until Sally pounced and chastised them for their rudeness, with a veiled motherly threat of no Christmas dinner if they didn't remove it. The little white plastic table by the back door had buckled under the weight of the snow that now sat on top of it. Polly could hardly wait to get out to the sumptuous comfort and cheeriness of the country, and of course, to see her sister again. She was also excited that her brothers Scott and Jared would be there too, all of them together again under one very accommodating roof.

"C'mon gang." Called Sally wafting the snow from Billy and Bruce's coats as they came in from the yard.

"Let's go!" Shouted Billy.

Polly was concerned as to the boys' manners today, yet felt content that Sally wouldn't allow them to get rude and silly at Maria's.

The bus took over an hour today, due to the weather up on the moors. But it wasn't a concern to this family and particularly to Polly as she wallowed in the vision before her, as the bus slowly made its way over the newly gritted roads. The drifts at the Fox House Inn on the moors resembled huge waves on an ocean of white, the air hung heavy over the pinnacle of Mam Tor. Where does it all go when it thaws? Polly silently asked herself.

Eventually the bus rounded to the terminus by the playing field, and the family climbed off, fastening their coats in preparation for the climb up the hill to the bungalow. They could see the lights of the Christmas tree through the window, twinkling as they grew nearer and nearer to warmth and comfort. Sally was gasping for air as she shuffled the final leg of her journey along Robert's shovelled and gritted driveway, the prize was the open door and Maria inviting her in with a warm pink glow behind her.

"Come on in Sally, I've a nice glass of mulled wine waiting for you."

"Oh," Sally gasped. "Ave you any oxygen love, it's like an expedition to the North Pole climbing that 'ill in this weather!"

Maria laughed and took Sally's coat. Libby was in the living room, also welcoming their guests, and while she was at it had a quiet word with Polly about how she thought Maria was overdoing things.

"She's acting a bit strange again." Whispered Libby, as they all sat down to the table. Wine was poured, there was the snap of crackers being pulled and happy conversation filled the house.

"Maria? You've laid too many places love" queried Sally.

"I'll 'ave it" called Billy.

"No, no!" Hesitated Maria, looking decidedly uncomfortable as though she had been caught out in some terrible subterfuge – which is exactly what it was. She continued. "We have an extra guest – or two, but erm', but they are a little late, must be the weather. Let's get started everyone! Tuck in!"

They were all enjoying the Christmas Fare laid before them; it was a banquet, a feast for the Gods, when there was a knock at the front door. The lulled conversation ceased abruptly, Silent Night continued on the Hi-fi, and everyone looked decidedly amazed at the interruption. Libby and Polly glanced nervously at one another and Maria excused herself to answer the door. Voices could be heard in the hallway, no-one spoke but sat with bated breath for this mystery guest to make an appearance. As the door opened, Maria entered with a hesitant smile.

"Here she is everyone!"

As she stepped aside to allow entry, in walked Grace Marsden. Of all people! Libby was now decidedly perplexed. She thought she had shaken off Social Services and Grace Marsden, lovely though she was. What *was* this all about? Libby was the first to speak, to break the silence.

"Hi Grace, nice to see you, I didn't know you had a baby" she queried.

Everyone was now staring, open, and empty mouthed at the child Grace was holding in her arms. A little boy aged about twelve or thirteen months, with dark curly hair and big brown dewy eyes.

"Sit down Grace, we've only just started" dithered Maria, as she began piling sprouts and parsnips onto the spare place-setting and Robert was nervously carving extra turkey.

"Well" began Grace. I don't have a baby, actually, of my own that is. This is someone else's baby, it's a new addition to *your* family and Maria and Robert have kindly decided to foster him."

Libby almost dropped her fork. Polly looked at her sister in horror. Libby rose from her seat and quietly said "Excuse me!" She fled to her room in tears. "How could they do this to me, on Christmas day of all days, or *ever* for that matter?"

There was a knock on Libby's door, and Maria quietly entered."

"Oh Libby, I'm so sorry. I didn't mean it to work out this way at all. *Please* come back to the table, we have more to tell you."

"*I* bet you have!" Sobbed Libby. "If you wanted me to leave, why didn't you just say so, when I turned eighteen? I know I'm not a cute little child anymore but I have feelings, and I'm *not* grown up at all!" And she hurled her face into her pillow." Maria decided alternative tactics were called for and she left the room and promptly returned with Grace close at her heels.

"Grace, could you talk to Libby please?" kicking herself for making such a mess of this. She had so wanted it to be 'good'.

"Of course." Said Grace softly. "Libby dear, I'm so, so sorry; Maria and I had no idea that you would get the wrong end of the stick. You see, she and I have been very busy, we wanted to surprise everyone and we thought it would be such a lovely Christmas present all round, and well, I'm usually alone on Christmas day and Maria kindly invited me to stay so I volunteered to do it today and, well ………..!" Gushing, was the only way to describe Grace's attempt at an explanation, so she decided to take the bull by the horns as it were.

"Look!" *You* are not going anywhere!"

Libby slid her face from beneath her crumpled pillow. She looked at Grace for a moment, and then flung her arms around her. She turned to Maria and silently repeated the gesture.

"Look at your face darling." Maria sobbed, stroking back the stray hairs which had adhered themselves to Libby's tear-stained face. Libby's eyeliner was now adorning her nose and her chin and her lip-gloss was transcending up her nostrils. Maria grasped a tissue from the dressing table and began the clean-up operation.

"Please come back in Libby." Pleaded Grace. "I have more to tell you."

All three women returned to the dining room. Everyone was still sitting there with no knowledge of what was happening. Polly had volunteered to hold the mystery baby, and found she was quite taken with him, and Sally was trying to control Billy and Bruce who were hurling sprouts across Maria's beautifully laid table.

"O.k. who's ready for pudding?" Called Maria with a smile and all the poise she could muster in her usual, well controlled manner.

As the meal continued, Robert brought in the Christmas pudding ablaze with brandy, with a sprig of holly from the garden atop it, and placed it in the centre of the table. At this point Maria decided to speak, as she rose from her seat and tapped her glass with a spoon, a hush descended.

"Well everyone, I really must apologise for the total mess I made of my surprise today, I was wrong for not taking feelings into consideration. It has been a very difficult year this year, Libby, Polly Scott and Jared, have had quite a shock, discovering the circumstances surrounding their father Darren and mum Tracey. Discovering one another also, has not been without its traumas and difficulties. However, today Grace and I wanted to present you with the piesté resistance to your dreams and wishes. May I present your youngest brother Max?" Maria extended her arm towards the beautiful little boy, smiling and gurgling on Polly's lap. A united gasp filled the air from all the guests, followed by happy shouting and hugging.

Maria plonked herself back on her chair with a gasp of relief and swigged back the remainder of the brandy Robert had left on the table. 'It turned out o.k. in the end.' She thought. The day rolled on in exuberant happiness, everyone was asking how this had been accomplished.

"Because Maria's amazing" interjected Libby. "Everything she does is unbelievable!"

Sally sat there nodding in agreement, with glass in hand and her cracker paper hat askew on her curly hair. Polly stood up and raised her glass of lemonade. "I wish to propose a toast to all our foster carers. They've been great, better than real parents to us and we can't thank them enough. "Three cheers!"

Sally smiled and blinked, and raised her glass, the wine and brandy now having its fully desired effect, as she could barely stand, her cheeks well flushed.

"Grace, is Max staying, now?" Asked Libby

"Absolutely! He's staying with you and Maria and Robert until Tracey is released from prison, and Maria has kindly agreed that all your brothers and sisters can come and visit him isn't that great?"

When all the frivolities were over, it was late into the evening and the table resembled a volcanic eruption, the turkey was no more than a skeleton and the paper hats had been turned into aeroplanes by Bruce and Billy, which had landed all over the dining room, Grace Marsden made her excuses and made ready to return to Sheffield. She offered Sally, John and the boys a lift, for which they were very grateful. Polly was staying for a few days and was now so very excited at the prospect of spending quality time with her new baby brother and of course her sister. Sally staggered out to Grace's car on the drive, firmly supported by John, and they all waved goodbye.

"I'll be back, after the holidays with some of Max's stuff." Called Grace as she manoeuvred the car out onto the icy lane.

Harriet and Fiona were staying the night and heading home in the morning. Scott and Jared left shortly after in Scott's barely roadworthy new acquisition, after lengthy cooing and cuddling with their little brother.

'What a day!' Thought Maria, as she flopped into Robert's easy chair and kicked off her black velvet slippers and poured herself another glass of wine.

"Go on" said Robert. "Relax a bit dear; you've done so well, all that planning's taken it out of you. I'll see to the baby and put him to bed.

Following the best night's sleep she'd had in ages Maria woke the next morning to Max's cries. He was hungry and wanted everyone to know. He wanted food, and he wanted it *now*! As she approached his cot, which was temporarily at the bottom of the bed, he greeted her with his toothy little grin. He appeared to like Maria and warmed to her immediately. Libby and Polly could hear him from Libby's room and smiled to each other at the thought of their little brother in the very next room to them.

'I don't need the sun to wake me anymore' she thought, 'I'll just wait for Max's food alert.' As they sat around the breakfast table on Boxing Day morning, Maria was overjoyed that all the family were together, what a rarity.

"Since we're all together this morning, there's something else I need to tell you'"

"Oh no!" Said Libby with her elbows on the table and her cupped hands beneath her chin. "Not another surprise Maria, I don't think I can take it!"

"Well dear, I think you'll like this one. I've decided I've had enough of the legal world. I'm taking early retirement to care for Max, *and* you of course. Max will stay here as long as needed. I also have the agreement to take Max to see Tracey, so that he will grow up knowing who his birth mother is, *and* of course his true brothers and sisters."

"Oh Maria, I can't thank you enough, you're the most wonderful person I have ever known."

Once more Maria walked out onto the balcony, her favourite thinking place. 'Hm, almost, *almost* not so wonderful' she thought. Maria knew she had pulled off

144

something quite remarkable, but she had learned many things along the way. She knew she couldn't have done any of it without Robert's support, or the devout input of Grace Marsden. My, how that woman had fought beaurocracy, how She and Grace, two women, had defied decisions made, and fought, gone one step further. Yet she was so pleased that their courage had reunited a family and that she had chosen to show empathy for Tracey and not to condemn her as so many had. Where there's a Will, there's a Woman! Now she hoped she could convince these siblings to give her a chance.

CHAPTER SEVENTEEN

Today, Tracey had something to smile about, she had been given the best Christmas gift she'd had in her entire life. Christmas had been little different to any other day, except for the food. Some reconstituted legless turkey, a portion of tinned carrots, frozen sprouts and tasteless gravy, followed by a small portion of very dry pudding. No glass of wine to assist its digestion, just the routine cup of sweet milky tea. Tracey was not complaining, she knew she deserved to be where she was, she was now realising that, whichever way you looked at it, she had taken someone's life, even a low-life like Darren, and restitution had to be made. At the beginning of her sentence she would have welcomed the theory of some – A Life for a Life and happily accepted the hangman's noose had it been available. But now, she had something to live for- Max, but also reconciliation with her older children if they had the capacity to forgive her for murdering their father.

Tracey was learning too, from recent events. She wished she'd had someone to guide and support her when she was young. Perhaps she wouldn't have leaned towards Darren for affection. She now also realised that Darren's affection was not true love, but rather lust, and when he tired of her, his selfish persona became more evident. One regret she did *not* have, was meeting Max senior and bearing his child, those memories would be forever with her each time she looked at baby Max, who was the image of his father. She did however regret taking Darren's life. No-one deserves to die, if only *he* had let her go, he didn't want her, but decided no-one else should have her either. She was also learning the value of foster care. She used to hate the very threat of going into care, and yet her life may have been very different if she had. *Now* she could see the value of people like Maria and Sally and their families, the loving determination of women with a purpose. She had been told today of the decision regarding her son. There had been a case conference about his future, and hers. Tracey had always known that her beloved Max would be placed in foster care but hoped with all her heart that they would not place him for adoption, to be lost to the system, perhaps forever, never to be seen by her again. She felt so desperate and out of control behind these bars. How on earth could she prove that she could be a good mother, given the chance, with the right support and under the right circumstances? She knew now that nothing would come before her son. She would sit in her cell and avoid any adverse behaviour, to ensure her sentence would be kept to a minimum. Christmas Day of all days, she kept herself, to herself. It was the season of Peace and Goodwill to all men, but that did not extend to the women in here. They were excluded from any of that by divine right, and therefore the usual cat-fights would ensue. The absence of alcohol made little difference; only a wrong glance was required in the wrong direction for a fight almost to the death, to follow.

Today, today was different, Tracey had had a visit from her social worker, who had informed her that the final case conference had taken place. She felt so useless; she had not been needed at *the* meeting which would decide the entire future of herself and her son. However, the news was good. In fact it was better than good, under the present circumstances, it was fantastic! She had been informed that Maria, the woman who wrote to her, who sounded so empathic and kind, who had shown her unconditional positive regard, was going to care for her son, until she was released, whenever that may be, she had not judged her. She prayed for her gratitude to be given to Grace Marsden for her co-operation. She thought of Grace and Maria as the Dynamic Duo, taking on the world. Once more, 'Where there's a Will, there's a Woman!' She reflected on the beautiful children she had given birth to and hoped with all her heart that they could find it in *their* hearts to forgive her for her actions.

As the New Year approached, there had been a meeting of the parole board, and they had considered Tracey's immaculate behaviour, heard of the situation regarding her children and her desire to be with them. Her case was under review and there was a good chance she may be given a reduced sentence. She had never had visitors, yet now she waited in anticipation of a visit from Maria with Max. Perhaps in the future, her children may find it in their hearts to become re-acquainted with her.

As she sat in her cell replying to Maria's letter, she smiled, a phenomenon which had become so alien to Tracey for so long. She had something to look forward to, at last. So moved was she that she felt compelled to write words from the heart. This is the poem she wrote:-

FEARS AND DREAMS

As I sit here alone, in my grey prison cell, I reminisce over my life

and my heart fills with pain.

I know *I* created my own private hell; all I ever wanted was sunshine,

but I got clouds filled with rain.

Within these four cold walls I languish, while the world outside is spinning by.

I'm emotionally soaked as I drown in my anguish, my wickedness I'll never deny.

No one *really* knows what I think, what I feel, I wanted so often

to take the world by the throat.

I never have known what to show, or conceal, while those all around me would gloat.

As a child I believed every dream would have wings, there'd be someone

beside me to calm all my fears.

To kiss my cheek 'till my beating heart would sing, but there was no joy to comfort me, and I drowned in angel's tears.

But when disappointment hoards my dreams, and floods my head with my sin,

I wish endless sleep would caress my senses and block my thoughts when I grieve.

Why can't I be carried in the arms of the angels and avoid the fools rushing in,

like a door with no key, and eyes that can't see, my head won't allow me to believe.

If only fate would step in through these grey prison walls,

I would cuddle the world with a wraparound hug,

as far as my arms would extend.

Softly, silently, as the white snow falls, fate would bring my hellish descent to an end,

I would crawl from the wreckage of my turbulent life,

from my dancing feet, you would tell.

I would flee from all anguish, trouble and strife, I would unchain my spirit from Hell!

Then behind me, I could put the endlessness of my past,

and bathe in the arms of my children, at last!

EPILOGUE

The little boy had just been to nursery, with his carer, full of energy he was excited at the prospect of going to the Fair and then to town for lunch.

"Can I have Candy Floss?" He called with continued excitement, as they hopped and skipped along after endless rides on Thomas the Tank, and going dizzy round and round in 'cups and saucers'.

As they entered the restaurant to be seated at the table which had been reserved, the waitress offered them a menu as she led them to the big round table by the window. Maria's 'phone rang.

"Oh Hi, yes I'm just about to have lunch with a friend, can I call you later?" She asked her caller. As she ended the conversation, she spotted her friend approaching from her vantage point by the window and waved and smiled.

"Mummy!" Yelled Max, as he flew to the door and into Tracey's open arms. There were tight, prolonged, whole body hugs, as Tracey held on to her son and kissed the top of his little head.

"Hi, Maria" She smiled. "Have you both had fun today at the Fair?"

"Yes!" Shrieked Max. "And Maria and me have had Candy Floss *and* Ice Cream."

"Not much room left for lunch then." Laughed Tracey. Max giggled. "Thanks so much for bringing him."

Maria smiled and touched Tracey's arm with a gentle reassuring squeeze and headed for the counter to request a coffee for her new friend. Max hopped and skipped around showing his mother his latest toy car.

It had taken a while but Tracey had finally been released on parole due to her excellent behaviour whilst in prison, keeping herself to herself had paid off. Over this time, she and Maria had become firm friends, their common goal being the welfare of Max. Maria laughed silently to herself, what would her solicitor friends make of this new acquaintance? The solicitor and the 'jailbird', a murderess no less, actually liked each other, and now of course, they had a common interest – Max junior! Here she was again, that 'Woman with a Will.' She just couldn't give up. She had been slowly assessing and monitoring Tracey's parenting skills, prompting her and guiding her, but more importantly, she had observed the natural bond of love grow between mother and child during the many visits they'd had with each other. Maria yet again, was a woman on a mission. It was soon to be Max's fifth birthday and she was arranging a party for him. No big secret this time. *Everyone* knew, and everyone was involved. Tracey could barely wait. All her children were going to be there, all of them together in one place, even Polly had agreed.

It had been a long and bumpy road for them all, for the children coming to terms with their past, learning to understand and forgive their mother, trying to get to grips with why they didn't grieve for their father, getting to know each other and their new brother Max. Max of course was as yet oblivious to the pain and grief which had been suffered by all those around him. That may have to be addressed in the future, but for now, he was enjoying being a little boy, loved by his mother and siblings, not to mention his foster carers, perhaps *this* would give him the security and stability he would need for the future. Tracey would be as honest as she could when the questions may come. She was currently concentrating on the day when Max would be handed over to her, to live with her, but of course she would always have Maria there to advise. Maria was the 'mother' she had never had, and she was relieved for herself and her son that Maria would be part of their lives. As for Maria, well, she now at last, felt ready to retire, like a grandmother with her brood around her. To fly off to the 'Island of Eternal Spring' once in a while and muse peacefully at the fluffy cloud formations hovering above volcano craters with no other responsibility than to ask herself why they did that.

Libby placed the last of the blue, car shaped candles on top of Max's birthday cake and wandered out onto the balcony. She gazed down at the little stone cottages below and focused on the main street through the village. She checked her watch; it was 2.25 p.m., time to begin her journey to meet Polly – and Tracey from the 2.30 p.m.

bus from Sheffield. Her Pandora's Box was now officially closed. Life was good!

One day at a time, this is enough.

Do not look back and grieve over the past for it is gone.

And do not be troubled about the future for it has not yet come.

Live in the present!

And make it so beautiful it will be worth remembering.

© COPYRIGHT 2013 HELD BY AUTHOR ALL RIGHTS RESERVED

Printed in Great Britain
by Amazon